WORLD HISTORY SERIES ■ ■ ■

The Cuban Revolution

Titles in the World History Series

WORLD HISTORY SERIES ▪▪▪

The Cuban Revolution

by
Earle Rice Jr.

Lucent Books, P.O. Box 289011, San Diego, CA 92198-9011

Library of Congress Cataloging-in-Publication Data

Rice, Earle
    The Cuban revolution / by Earle Rice, Jr.
       p. cm.—(World history series)
    Includes bibliographical references and index.
    ISBN 1-56006-275-4 (alk. paper)
    1. Castro, Fidel, 1927-   —Juvenile literature. 2. Cuba—
History—1933-1959—Juvenile literature. 3. Cuba—History—
Revolution, 1959—Juvenile literature. 4. Cuba—History—1959-
—Juvenile literature. 5. Cuba—History—Revolution, 1959.
[1. Castro, Fidel, 1927- . 2. Cuba—History—1933-1959.
3. Cuba—History—1959- .]   I.Title. II. Series.
F1788.22.C3R5   1995
972.9106'4—dc20   94-26604
                                     CIP
                                     AC

Copyright 1995 by Lucent Books, Inc., P.O. Box 289011,
San Diego, California, 92198-9011

Printed in the U.S.A.

Contents

Foreword

Each year on the first day of school, nearly every history teacher faces the task of explaining why his or her students should study history. One logical answer to this question is that exploring what happened in our past explains how the things we often take for granted—our customs, ideas, and institutions—came to be. As statesman and historian Winston Churchill put it, "Every nation or group of nations has its own tale to tell. Knowledge of the trials and struggles is necessary to all who would comprehend the problems, perils, challenges, and opportunities which confront us today." Thus, a study of history puts modern ideas and institutions in perspective. For example, though the founders of the United States were talented and creative thinkers, they clearly did not invent the concept of democracy. Instead, they adapted some democratic ideas that had originated in ancient Greece and with which the Romans, the British, and others had experimented. An exploration of these cultures, then, reveals their very real connection to us through institutions that continue to shape our daily lives.

Another reason often given for studying history is the idea that lessons exist in the past from which contemporary societies can benefit and learn. This idea, although controversial, has always been an intriguing one for historians. Those that agree that society can benefit from the past often quote philosopher George Santayana's famous statement, "Those who cannot remember the past are condemned to repeat it." Historians who ascribe to Santayana's philosophy believe that, for example, studying the events that led up to the major world wars or other significant historical events would allow society to chart a different and more favorable course in the future.

Just as difficult as convincing students to realize the importance of studying history is the search for useful and interesting supplementary materials that present historical events in a context that can be easily understood. The volumes in Lucent Books' World History Series attempt to present a broad, balanced, and penetrating view of the march of history. Ancient Egypt's important wars and rulers, for example, are presented against the rich and colorful backdrop of Egyptian religious, social, and cultural developments. The series engages the reader by enhancing historical events with these cultural contexts. For example, in *Ancient Greece*, the text covers the role of women in that society. Slavery is discussed in *The Roman Empire*, as well as how slaves earned their freedom. The numerous and varied aspects of everyday life in these and other societies are explored in each volume of the series. Additionally, the series covers the major political, cultural, and philosophical ideas as the torch of civilization is passed from ancient Mesopotamia and Egypt, through Greece, Rome, Medieval Europe, and other world cultures, to the modern day.

The material in the series is formatted in a thorough, precise, and organized manner. Each volume offers the reader a comprehensive and clearly written overview of an important historical event or period. The topic under discussion is placed in a broad, historical context. For example, *The Italian Renaissance* begins with a discussion of the High Middle Ages and the loss of central control that allowed certain Italian cities to develop artistically. The book ends by looking forward to the Reformation and interpreting the societal changes that grew out of the Renaissance. Thus, students are not only involved in an historical era, but also enveloped by the events leading up to that era and the events following it.

One important and unique feature in the World History Series is the primary and secondary source quotations that richly supplement each volume. These quotes are useful in a number of ways. First, they allow students access to sources they would not normally be exposed to because of the difficulty and obscurity of the original source. The quotations range from interesting anecdotes to far-sighted cultural perspectives and are drawn from historical witnesses both past and present. Second, the quotes demonstrate how and where historians themselves derive their information on the past as they strive to reach a consensus on historical events. Lastly, all of the quotes are footnoted, familiarizing students with the citation process and allowing them to verify quotes and/or look up the original source if the quote piques their interest.

Finally, the books in the World History Series provide a detailed launching point for further research. Each book contains a bibliography specifically geared toward student research. A second, annotated bibliography introduces students to all the sources the author consulted when compiling the book. A chronology of important dates gives students an overview, at a glance, of the topic covered. Where applicable, a glossary of terms is included.

In short, the series is designed not only to acquaint readers with the basics of history, but also to make them aware that their lives are a part of an ongoing human saga. Perhaps they will then come to the same realization as famed historian Arnold Toynbee. In his monumental work, *A Study of History,* he wrote about becoming aware of history flowing through him in a mighty current, and of his own life "welling like a wave in the flow of this vast tide."

Important Dates in the History of the Cuban Revolution

1492	1520	1560	1600	1640	1680	1720

1492
Christopher Columbus sails along northeastern coast of Cuba and establishes Spain's claim of possession.

1511-15
The conquistador Diego de Velásquez lands in Cuba. Chief Hatuey of the Guahaba Indians burned at the stake by the Spaniards. Spain's conquest of Cuba completed within four years.

1602-1607
First colonial rebellion against Spanish authority over government attempt to ban illegal goods. Havana established as capital in 1607.

1728
University of Havana founded.

1789
Spanish Crown authorizes free slave trade.

1811-12
José Antonio Aponte, a free black, leads uprising to end slavery.

1817
Pact between Spain and England ends slavery.

1851
Rebellions against annexation put down in May and July.

1853
José Julian Martí is born.

1868-78
Ten Years' War begins in Oriente province on October 10, 1868. Rebellion expands across Oriente into Camagüey and Las Villas provinces. Pact of Zanjón ends war on May 21, 1878.

1879-80
The "Little War," led by Gen. Calixto García, breaks out in Oriente in August 1879 and ends nine months later.

1895
Second war for independence begins on February 24. José Martí killed in May. In October, forces led by Antonio Maceo and Máximo Gómez invade western provinces.

1896
Antonio Maceo killed in battle in December.

1898
The Spanish-American War begins and ends 114 days later. Cuban sovereignty transferred to the United States by Paris Peace Treaty signed by the United States and Spain in December.

1900-1901
The United States enacts the Platt Amendment. Tomás Estrada Palma elected as first Cuban president.

1903
The United States and Cuba sign three treaties, notably the Permanent Treaty that invokes the Platt Amendment.

1906-1909
Following the "August Revolution" in 1906, the U.S. military occupies and governs Cuba at the request of Estrada Palma.

1912-22
Mario G. Menocal elected president in 1912. The "February Revolution" of 1917 provokes a second U.S. intervention. The U.S. troops remain in Cuba until 1922.

1924
Gerardo Machado elected to first term as president.

1933
Military coup ousts Machado and installs Carlos Manuel de Céspedes as president. Fulgencio Batista leads "Revolt of the Sergeants'" in September. Céspedes overthrown and replaced by Ramón Grau San Martín for one hundred days.

1934
Batista overthrows Grau and installs Carlos Mendieta as president in January. The United States voids Platt Amendment in May. Grau and others organize the Auténtico Party.

| 1760 | 1800 | 1840 | 1880 | 1920 | 1960 | 1993 |

1936
Miguel Mariano Gómez takes office as president. Batista replaces him with Federico Laredo Bru after twelve months.

1938
Communist Party recognized in Cuba as legal organization.

1940
The constitution of Cuba adopted. Fulgencio Batista elected president.

1944
Ramón Grau San Martín elected president as Auténtico Party candidate.

1948
Carlos Prío Socarrás becomes president for four-year term.

1952
Fulgencio Batista seizes power by military force, ousts Prío, and ends constitutional government in Cuba.

1953
Fidel Castro and followers attack Moncada Barracks in Santiago on July 26. Attack fails and survivors sentenced to long prison terms.

1955
Batista declares amnesty for Moncada attackers. Fidel Castro and members of the new 26th of July Movement depart for Mexico.

1956
Fidel Castro returns to Cuba and commences guerrilla operations against Batista in the Sierra Maestra.

1957
Fidelistas launch first successful attack at La Plata in January. In March, the Revolutionary Directorate (DR) attack the Presidential Palace in Havana. DR leader José Antonio Echeverría killed in failed attempt to assassinate Batista.

1958
Raúl Castro establishes second guerrilla front in the Sierra Cristal. General strike fails to oust Batista. Government forces routed in rebel counterattack. Batista flees Cuba on New Year's Eve.

1959
Rebels take power. Fidel Castro arrives in Havana on January 8. Agrarian Reform Bill enacted in May.

1960
Cuba reestablishes relations with the Soviet Union and nationalizes North American properties on the island.

1961
The United States severs relations with Cuba in January. In April, Cuban expatriot invasion fails at Bay of Pigs.

1962
Cuban Missile Crisis, October 22-28.

1967
Ernesto "Che" Guevara killed in Bolivia in October.

1970
"Ten-Million-Ton" sugar harvest falls short at 8.5 million tons. Cuban economy falters.

1975
Cuba sends combat troops to join Angola's fight for liberation against Portugal.

1978-79
The United States and Cuba open limited relations. Cuba starts program to reunite families of Cuban exiles.

1980
Mariel boatlift emigrates 125,000 Cubans to Miami.

1983
The United States intervenes in Grenada.

1987
Cuba agrees to accept return of two thousand "undesirable" Cubans. In return, the United States agrees to accept twenty thousand new Cuban immigrants each year.

1993
Fidel Castro remains as Cuba's leader. Cuba's relations with the United States remain unfriendly.

Born to Change History

Cuba's Fidel Castro has always been fond of saying that he was born to change history. He has repeatedly voiced this opinion of himself in a matter-of-fact way.

During one recorded interview, he said, "Since I didn't come from a family of politicians or grow up in a political atmosphere, it would have been impossible for me to carry out a revolutionary role . . . in a relatively brief time, had I not had a special calling."[1] Whether by fate or by chance, he has backed his words with deeds. Few have changed history more.

Beginning in the early 1950s, the face and shape of Cuba were altered forever by the Cuban Revolution. Fidel Castro, more than any other person, provided the life's breath and driving force for change. This is the story of that revolution. It is also the story of Fidel Castro, for it is impossible to separate the two.

Cuba's "Maximum Leader"

Since 1959, Fidel has served as *el líder máximo*—the "maximum leader"—of Cuba. The changes that have taken place there since 1959 occurred, for the most part, at his will and under his direction. And so it is that both credit and blame for the state of Cuba today must reside with him. It is from that notion that this account evolves.

But what of the other forces at work, both inside and outside Cuba? What lit the flame of unrest and set the fires of rebellion burning across this small island nation? Revolution is a difficult and deadly game at best. Few who play it ever win. So just what were the elements of chance, time, and place that came together to enable Fidel and his followers to succeed?

Fidel Castro speaks to crowds following the 1959 coup. Castro inspired the Cuban Revolution, both as its author and enforcer.

More than forty years have passed since the start of the Cuban Revolution; yet historians, scholars, political analysts, world leaders and policy makers, and serious thinkers everywhere still debate its causes. Most experts agree, however, on at least three major factors that were present in Cuba during this latest period of unrest: (1) political repression, (2) economic imbalance and depression, and (3) a perceived threat by some Cubans of "Yankee imperialism," resulting from the uneven policies of the United States toward Cuba since 1898.

Many other factors added to the sum of Cuba's discontent immediately before the revolution. Some of the more important ones, along with the three principal factors, are examined in the pages to follow.

Although factors create a cradle for revolution, factors do not revolt; people revolt. Therefore, there must be a government in place to revolt *against*. It is usually one that the people see as repressive, unjust, inept, or corrupt. As Fidel and his young rebels started down the road to revolution, the government in power appeared to qualify on all counts. It was headed by a self-proclaimed president who rose from humble beginnings as an army sergeant to become the "strongman of Cuba."

Three weeks before the 1952 Cuban presidential elections, Gen. Fulgencio Batista Zaldívar—a former president, and once again a candidate for that office—was running third in a three-man race. Dr. Roberto Agramonte of the Ortodoxos Party led in all the polls, followed by Dr. Aurelio Hevia of the Auténtico Party. At this point, Batista decided to turn a likely political defeat into a sudden, stunning victory. He simply seized control of the government by force of arms.

Fulgencio Batista (center) was a military general before he seized the Cuban government to become president. Under his rule, Cuba went from a democracy to a military dictatorship.

Batista Takes Over

In the early morning of March 10, 1952, Batista and a handful of fellow officers entered Camp Columbia in Havana—Cuba's largest military installation—and took control of the Cuban army. With the army supporting him, he overthrew the presidency of Carlos Prío Socarrás in a scant seventy-seven minutes. Only two men died in Batista's almost bloodless takeover, and an indifferent nation seemed neither to notice nor to care. Insofar as the citizens of Cuba were concerned, it was business as usual.

By late that afternoon, Batista, the old army sergeant, was firmly in power. Prío fled the country a few hours later. He left the control and destiny of Cuba in the grasping hands of the latest in a long line of iron-fisted leaders.

Before Batista's takeover, Cuba's government had still functioned as a democracy. Government offices, however, were riddled with graft and corruption from top to bottom. Still, Cubans held to the hope that by electing the right leadership a democratic government might yet be preserved. Batista's sudden strike slammed the door shut on the hopes of most of them.

Doorway to Revolution

Fidel Castro, however, looked far beyond the event of March 10, and his hopes sprang alive: He saw not the closing of the door to democracy but rather the opening of the door to revolution. "If anyone was responsible for opening the way to Cas-

Wanted: A Man to Make the Revolution

Although conditions in Cuba were ripe for revolt at the time Batista resumed control of the government, a revolution was not likely. Most Cubans, according to Herbert L. Matthews in his book Fidel Castro, *were willing to shrug their shoulders and accept the Batista government. Only one man felt strongly enough to do something about it.*

"Batista's coup provided Fidel with an excuse for action, but anyone who was in Cuba at the time, as I was, could not help being struck by the fact that those who felt disgust and anger were a minority with no possibility or intention of revolting. The vast majority of Cubans shrugged their shoulders and took the *cuartelazo*, or garrison revolt, philosophically: 'There's that man again.' [The revolt installed Batista as head of the Cuban government for the second time.]

Only one Cuban felt strongly enough and had the leadership qualities to do something about it. What he did—the Moncada Barracks attack on July 26, 1953—seemed futile at the time and it was rash to the point of madness, but that is how the man of destiny makes history.

Fidel Castro was rebelling against a system, a society, a corrupt and rotten state of affairs that spawned men like Fulgencio Batista. He was rebelling, too, against an economic structure run largely by foreigners, against income inequalities and high and growing unemployment. Deep inside of him and of all Cubans was a revolutionary tradition inherited from the decades of struggle against Spain, nourished in this century by continual United States military interventions.

There were reasons enough for a revolution whether Batista had come along or not. What was needed was a man to make the revolution."

Castro, still leader of his country, speaks to crowds in 1992. Although much criticism has been leveled at his rule, Castro remains a phenomenal figure in what he has accomplished.

tro's capture of power, that man was Fulgencio Batista."[2]

With a vision that history grants only to a few, Fidel saw himself as Cuba's savior. He began at once to prepare for the role. Over the next seven years, he forged and led the movement that eventually overthrew Batista. In early 1959, he unseated the dictator and installed himself as Premier of Cuba.

Once in power, Fidel turned Cuba away from a democracy to embrace communism—or *Castroism*. Overall the Cuban economy has suffered under Fidel. Improvements in public health care, education, and agriculture seem to represent his only major gains. Still, he maintains a large military and continues to attempt to export his revolution to other Third World countries. In 1962, he moved the world to the brink of nuclear war by installing Soviet nuclear missiles in Cuba. His role in President John F. Kennedy's assassination remains unclear even today. What is clear is the major impact Fidel has had, not only on Cuba, but on the entire world.

At this writing, Fidel Castro continues to rule. But his days as Cuba's *líder máximo* grow short. His role in Cuba and the world must await the judgment of future generations. Whether history acclaims or condemns his performance, at least one thing seems certain: His legacy will remain.

1 Moncada: The Birth of the 26th of July Movement

"A revolution is not the same as inviting people to dinner, or writing an essay, or painting a picture. . . . A revolution is an insurrection, an act of violence by which one class overthrows another."

—Mao Tse-tung
Report, March 1927, in *Selected Works* (1954) vol. 1, p. 27

It was a summer madness. Or so it would seem. But beyond the madness there burned in the hearts and minds of all who took part a flame of idealism, patriotism, selflessness, and courage seldom imagined in the most heroic of fictions. Their truth was to be a story written in bravery, brashness, and blood. It was a summer madness that began the Cuban Revolution.

On the eve of July 26, 1953, they came to the fabled beach of Siboney, and to the historic old city of Santiago, the capital of Oriente province. They arrived in the company of a carnival atmosphere and an oppressive summer heat, noble of purpose and determined to succeed. They came singly and in pairs, from all around the is-

Fidel Castro with his followers, or Fidelistas. Castro was able to give masses of Cubans a sense of purpose and shared goals.

land, and from all sectors of the society. Numbering around one hundred, their numbers pale in the light of history, but their epic deeds remain sharply clear and unforgettable. They called themselves *Fidelistas*—the revolutionary disciples of Fidel Alejandro Castro Ruz. They came to Siboney and Santiago, and to Moncada, an old army barracks, to execute Castro's plan to overthrow the Batista government by force of arms. And they came prepared to die, if necessary, in the pursuit of freedom. This is their story.

It is fitting to say at the outset that the story of the Cuban Revolution and the life of Fidel Castro cannot be separated. In a very real sense, one *is* the other: a wedding of the right moment in time with the perfect personality to seize that moment.

Herbert L. Matthews, a distinguished reporter for the *New York Times* and an early biographer of Fidel, keenly observed:

> One cannot make sense out of the Cuban Revolution without keeping in mind at all times the personal supremacy—at first potential and then real—of Fidel Castro. This predominance can be seen in its embryonic stage in the fervent response of the young men and women who surrounded him, or who were drawn to him by his magnetic personality.[3]

Of those drawn to Fidel by his "magnetic personality" in the earliest stage of his revolt, only a handful formed the core of his yet-to-be-named movement. Notable among the earliest and more select members of Fidel's core group were Abel Santamaría, his deputy, an accountant at a Havana Pontiac dealer's office; Jesús Montané Oropesa, Abel's friend, also an accountant; Haydée (Yeyé) Santamaría,

Abel's sister; Dr. Melba Hernández, a woman attorney; and forty-five-year-old Dr. Mario Muñoz, a Havana physician, the only member of the Moncada group older than age thirty. Ernesto Tizol, a Miami restaurant owner, and Pedro Miret, a Havana engineer, joined them in early 1952, as did a number of others. Raúl Castro, Fidel's younger brother, became one of the last to join the movement on his return from a students' tour of Europe in July 1953. The birth of Fidel's movement had begun fifteen months earlier.

Batista Overthrows Prío Government

On March 10, 1952, Gen. Fulgencio Batista mounted an unexpected coup d'état—the sudden overthrow of a government by force—against President Carlos Prío Socarrás. Batista had seized control of the army by a similar act against the Machado government in 1933, using this strength to become president of Cuba in 1940. He had voluntarily stepped down in 1944 but had grown to like the power of the presidency so much that he now took it back by force. His first rule had been bad but not all bad. This time he was to rule not as president but as dictator, maintaining his office through violence and repression.

Batista's March 10 coup, in the words of Fidel's biographer Georgie Anne Geyer, "marked the beginning of the Fidel Castro the world would come to know. From that day, he would begin the organization of his own first 'movement.'"[4]

Fidel immediately dedicated himself to Batista's removal by whatever means necessary. He tried first to force Batista from power by legal means, as Geyer further notes:

> Within days, Fidel had filed a brief in the Court of Constitutional Guarantees to try to force what was left of the Cuban legal system to declare Batista's seizure of power to be unconstitutional. He asked "modestly" that the man who in effect held total power in the country be sentenced to one hundred years in prison.[5]

Fidel's brief invoked the Cuban Constitution of 1940, supposedly the legitimate law of the land. He soon recognized, however, that it would take more than a court appeal to remove Batista. Acting in its own self-interest, the court declined to try Batista, but by filing the brief Fidel established a legal base for his planned revolution. He could now justify it as a legal act against an illegal government. There was more than one way to attack the problem.

In absolute secrecy, Fidel set about forming an organization of loyal followers who shared his dedication and zeal for the difficult and dangerous task ahead. They numbered few at first, barely ten; but according to Melba Hernández, who spoke in glowing terms about their leader, "we felt like a movement of tremendous force. He had been born. We were born with him."[6] Her words offered a clear indication of the spell cast by Fidel over his followers.

They met clandestinely on a weekly basis. Many of their meetings took place in the small house of Abel and Haydée Santamaría at O and 25th in Havana. The town of Artemisa to the west of Havana, on the way to Pinar del Rio, served as another key meeting place. Its rural setting offered ideal conditions for military training. So, the young rebels met, and planned, and trained over the course of many months, adding steadily to their numbers, while preparing to change their world.

Through it all, Fidel remained a shadowy figure, always present yet never visibly associated with his followers. Despite his low profile, he directed every move and nuance of the movement, much as a motion-picture director controls all the action from behind the camera. All of Cuba—and the world—would know of Fidel Castro soon enough. And his name would be forever linked with the events of a midsummer's morn at Cuartel Moncada in Santiago in Cuba's easternmost province of Oriente.

The Moncada Plan

Moncada is the second largest military installation in Cuba, Camp Columbia in Havana being the largest. Although Fidel probably carried the idea of an attack on the Moncada barracks in his head for many months, the first serious plotting began in February of 1953. He and Abel Santamaría leased an old farmhouse on a two-acre chicken ranch near Siboney Beach, ten minutes from downtown Santiago. Because of its location next to the famous beach—a favorite resort of vacationers—they aptly named it "El Siboney," and established the ranch as their headquarters. From there they sent handpicked men into Santiago itself to rent apartments and begin an around-the-clock watch on Moncada. Bit by bit, under tight security, they fashioned a battle plan, allowing only six key individuals to know its details.

Back in Havana and other points around the island, the *Fidelistas* pursued a host of tasks essential to the success of the impending attack. They raised money, gathered arms and ammunition, sewed Cuban army uniforms—to be worn they knew not where—and more. None of them would receive the slightest hint as to the gravity of Fidel's plan until the eve of its execution.

Of the plan, Haydée Santamaría said, simply, "We had no idea what 'Moncada' would be, but it didn't matter, because in any case it would be 'Moncada.'"[7] Indeed it would.

The plan itself, though bold and dangerous, held more than a little worth in a strategic sense. But it would require perfect execution and a lot of luck. On the evening of July 25, 1953, with all of his volunteers present at El Siboney, Fidel stood tall among them and dramatically outlined his plan. He finished to an audience gripped in silence, as if no one dared to breathe. Finally, Gustavo Arcos commented that the plan was suicidal, provoking Fidel to accuse him of cowardice. Arcos' response left no doubt as to his courage.

In the tradition of Cuban romantics before him, he said, "I will go to Moncada even if I die." He paused and went on, "I hope that you are willing to die, too."[8] He might have been one of only a few who understood what was really happening. Dr. Mario Muñoz, older and more mature than the rest, was another.

"Fidel, I am ready to die for Cuba," the doctor said then, "but to think that we can take the Moncada barracks with a few more than a hundred men, when they have a garrison of more than a thousand soldiers, is to send these boys to a sure suicide."[9]

This enraged Fidel, who fiercely resented challenges to his authority. He started to tell Muñoz that he could stay behind, but Muñoz interrupted him. He said that he would be among the first to fight, but repeated that the plan seemed to him "to be madness, even a crime."[10] Fidel didn't answer.

At this point, to the ire and disgust of Fidel, ten of the *Fidelistas* withdrew from further participation in the Moncada affair. Their leader promptly banished them to the bathroom until the others departed. The rest gathered close and together sang the Cuban national anthem in

In Havana, the Fidelistas *prepared for the attack on Moncada by raising money, gathering weapons, and sewing uniforms.*

The Batista Coup

From the moment Fidel Castro heard about the Batista coup, he knew that a "new revolutionary cycle" had begun in Cuba. In her book Guerrilla Prince: The Untold Story of Fidel Castro, *Georgie Anne Geyer describes the coup that started Fidel on his revolutionary path to power.*

"The coup d'état that changed Cuban history took place at 2:43 A.M. that Monday, March 10, [1952] when General Fulgencio Batista, wearing a leather jacket and packing a .45 caliber pistol, strode into Camp Columbia and took command of the army. In a mere seventy-seven minutes, it was all over. The *Batistianos* held control of the army, the navy, and the air force, and that was all it took to destroy 'democracy' in Cuba. By midday, Batista was in power, and Carlos Prío had fled the palace and, soon, the country, to settle in Mexico. The coup d'état in Cuba did not seem very serious to a world occupied by larger questions. Only two men died that day, and not even the movie theaters closed to mark the moment. The exultant Batista crowed, 'My destiny is to carry out revolutions without bloodshed.' If the Americans had listened more carefully, they would have heard Batista say after the coup, 'The people and I are the dictators.' The similarity to words spoken by strongmen Juan Perón [Argentine dictator] and Jorge Eliecer Gaitán [Colombian political reformist] was astounding!"

The longer Fulgencio Batista ruled Cuba, the more dictatorial he became. His overthrow seemed inevitable.

voices barely above a whisper, then fell silent to await the dawn.

No Turning Back

In the gray moments before sunrise, the *Fidelistas* loaded into vehicles and formed a convoy of twenty-six cars. All wore the uniforms of Cuban army sergeants. At precisely 5:00 A.M., Fidel, in the second car, issued the order to depart. The first car, with Renato Guitart—who lived in Santiago and was to lead the attack—headed out of El Siboney and onto the road to Santiago. The others followed in column, on their way to a variety of awesome destinies. Many would not survive the day.

As described by author Tad Szulc:

The Moncada barracks is an ugly sprawl of buildings and fields in the shape of an irregular rectangle, occupying a 15-acre area of high ground in downtown Santiago. It was originally built as a fortress by the Spaniards and reconstructed after a fire in 1938. Named for General Guillermo Moncada of the Liberation Army in the independence wars, following the establishment of the Cuban republic, it served an essentially internal security function inasmuch as an external attack on Santiago was wholly unlikely [that is, it was used as a base for maintaining civil order rather than for defending against invasion from abroad].[11]

Fidel and his coconspirators planned their attack for early Sunday morning, reasoning that revelers celebrating at the annual Carnival of Santería the night before—many of whom were soldiers from Moncada—

would be sleeping in. They reasoned correctly. As the convoy entered the city and moved toward the fort, it barely received a lifted eyebrow. Their luck held as they wound their way through the cobbled streets, moving ever closer to Moncada.

Szulc continues:

The Moncada compound was divided into two main parts. The eastern portion of the rectangle was a firing range, the western portion was the fort proper—the objective of the rebel operation. The fort's perimeter was formed by thick-walled, two-story crenellated [notched] yellow barracks buildings on its east side, where the official entrance to Moncada headquarters was located, as well as along the

A youthful Fidel Castro in 1953. Fidel was personally involved in every aspect of the revolution.

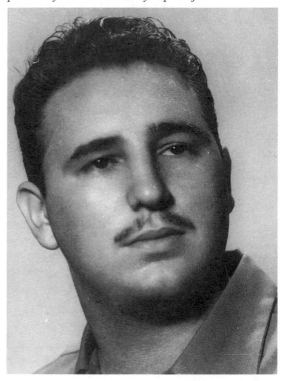

south and north sides for a half-block each. The other half-blocks on the northern and southern flanks and the entire length of the western side of the compound were protected by high walls and fences.[12]

The moment of attack on the army barracks at Moncada was set for 5:15 A.M., as was a similar attack on Bayamo, one hundred miles northwest of Santiago; they were carried out almost to the second at both installations. Renato Guitart's lead car, the "suicide" car, pulled into Mon-

cada's Gate 3 at the appointed time. The uniformed Guitart, Jesús Montané, and Ramiro Valdés slid out of the front seat and stepped briskly toward the sentry box. The sentries watched them idly with no outward sign of alarm. Valdés disconnected and cleared away the heavy chain across the roadway. Simultaneously, Guitart and Montané called the sentries to attention, shouting, "The General is coming!"

The ploy worked. Before the sentries realized what was happening, the business end of pistols jammed into their midriffs

The Moncada Plan

The first overt blow struck by Fidel Castro in the name of a free Cuba came at the Moncada barracks in Santiago de Cuba, in the early morning of July 26, 1953. In M-26, Biography of a Revolution, *author Robert Taber describes the essential elements of Castro's daring plan to overthrow the regime of Fulgencio Batista.*

"His [Castro's] purpose was to seize the armory with all speed, exchange the shotguns and light sporting rifles with which his untried revolutionaries were armed for military weapons, broadcast an appeal to the people, and proceed at once to establish a popular militia in support of the revolutionary government, with Santiago as its capital.

A coordinated attack in the city of Bayamo, one hundred miles to the west and north of Santiago, was intended as the essential first step toward establishing advanced outposts along the strategic river Cauto, to repel any invasion from the western provinces.

The uprising was not, then, at least not in its conception, a mere suicide attack prompted by psychological and political motives, but an open declaration of war against an illegitimate military regime. Nor was the plan of operations as impractical as it has been made to appear. It came within an ace of succeeding. It may be as well that it did not, for it could have split Oriente [province] off from the rest of the country and plunged Cuba into a bloody civil war for which it was then totally unprepared."

persuaded them to surrender their weapons. So far, so good.

At the same time, fourteen rebels in two cars, led by Abel Santamaría, Fidel's second-in-command, proceeded toward the Civil Hospital across the street from the fort. Once inside, Dr. Muñoz was to direct preparations for receiving casualties, with Melba Hernández and Haydée Santamaría serving as nurses.

In the meantime, Fidel, following behind Guitart, had been held up at an intersection by a chance encounter with a two-man army patrol with machine guns and an armed sergeant. Historian Hugh Thomas described what happened next this way:

> Castro ran his car against the machine gunners and the sergeant fled. But he [the sergeant] could clearly give the alarm. Following previous orders, once Castro's car stopped, the men in the following cars all leapt out and attacked the buildings [dormitories containing soldiers sleeping in after a night of celebration] to their left. Castro tried unsuccessfully to regroup his men. Inside the barracks, the men of the first car, having bewildered a dormitory of undressed soldiers, found themselves cut off, and having shot down a number of sergeants, as well as the officer of the day, Lieutenant Morales, withdrew. The alarm being given, a general fusillade followed from the first floors into the street.[13]

Fidelistas Suffer Defeat

Meanwhile, Raúl Castro and his group captured the poorly defended Palace of

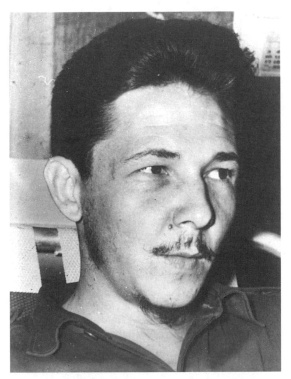

Fidel's brother, Raúl Castro, was also heavily involved in the revolution. He led his own division during the attack on Moncada.

Justice, while Abel Santamaría's party secured the Civil Hospital. Both objectives were taken with no losses to the *Fidelistas* or to the army. But the element of surprise was lost. The assault then evolved into a huge mismatch between a hundred or so disorganized rebels armed with small-caliber weapons, and a highly disciplined, heavily armed force of possibly one thousand soldiers.

The defeat of Fidel and his followers became virtually assured when a reserve force lost its way in the spiderwebbed streets of Santiago. Ironically, as recorded by Georgie Anne Geyer:

> The ten men who had refused to go to the fight did not stay in the bathroom

at the ranch as they had been instructed. Instead, they left the house, and in driving away they inadvertently drifted into the line of cars heading for Moncada. Making a wrong turn, they led those fighters behind them, who did not know Santiago, into the city. So, as the real battle began, the men who were to back up Fidel and his group in the crucial attack on Post [Gate] 3 were haplessly wandering the streets trying to find the second largest military garrison in Cuba![14]

The Aftermath

When Fidel recognized defeat, he quickly called for a retreat. He and his men withdrew, leaving wounded and others behind to be captured. Renato Guitart "was killed in front of Gate 3, along with Pedro Marrero, Carmelo Noa, and Flores Betancourt. They were the first rebel fatalities of Castro's revolution."[15] Many more would follow.

Raúl Castro and his men watched the withdrawal from high atop the terrace of the Palace of Justice, unable to help. With defeat imminent, they managed to escape by simply removing their uniforms and nonchalantly disappearing into the streets of Santiago in their civilian clothes. The twenty rebels occupying the Civil Hospital enjoyed no such luck.

Fidel later told Carlos Franqui, diarist of the Cuban Revolution:

Only one of our group was killed in the hospital. The rest were cornered when the troops blocked the only exit from the building, and only laid down their arms when the ammunition ran out. Abel Santamaría, the most beloved and daring of all our young men was with them. His glorious part in the resistance movement will find a place in the history of Cuba.[16]

At about 8:00 A.M., the sounds of the gun battle going on outside dropped off and became sporadic. This was not a good sign for the rebels. Abel called aside his sister Haydée and Melba Hernández and said:

We've had it. You know what is going to happen to me, and perhaps to everybody: but it's more important not to risk you two. Hide in the hospital and just wait. You have a much better chance than anybody else of staying alive—do that, at all costs. Somebody has to survive to tell what really happened here.[17]

The two women then lost track of Abel in the confusion of conflict but saw him a few minutes later in the courtyard below. They looked on as Batista troops arrested him and smashed him with rifle butts before leading him away. Dr. Muñoz, one of the few *Fidelistas* who seemed to know what he was getting into, was caught and shot in the back by his captors. He lay where he fell, in a congealing pool of his own blood, for hours.

Later, in the basement of the Santiago police station, a sergeant came to the cell where Haydée and Melba were being held after their capture. He showed Haydée a bleeding eyeball that he held in his hand and said, "This belongs to your brother, and if you don't tell us what he refused to tell us, we'll gouge his other one out too." Although she loved her brother more than anything else in the world, she managed to answer, "If he didn't tell you anything when you gouged his eye out, you will get less out of me."[18] The same man later returned and told her that Batista's soldiers had killed her brother.

Fidel and eighteen others escaped into the Sierra Maestra, where they were caught and imprisoned several days later. Brother Raúl headed north toward the Castro home in Birán. But he too was caught and returned to Santiago for trial.

The twenty-seven *Fidelistas* who attacked the army barracks at Bayamo met with similar failures and consequences. Two of their bodies were found hanged alongside the Manzanillo highway; three others, at the bottom of a well. At least ten rebel prisoners were killed before a priest intervened. Those who remained stood trial.

Fidel's movement—which would soon become known as the "26th of July Movement," or simply, the "M-26-7" or "M-26"— suffered severe losses. Enraged by the Moncada attack, the Batista government issued an order to exact payment for its casualties in the amount of ten rebel lives for every one dead soldier. The *Batistianos* complied with gusto. All in all, more than one hundred *Fidelistas* were murdered or captured. A three-judge Provisional Tribunal of Santiago—a special political court whose sentences could not be appealed—would administer Cuban justice to the survivors.

Fidel Explains Moncada Failure

The best-armed half of the attackers got lost and wasn't in position at the vital moment; and Fidel's car ran into an army patrol, which alerted the garrison too soon. But tactical mistakes were also committed. Fidel later explained these mistakes to Carlos Franqui, who relates them in his book Diary of the Cuban Revolution.

"I think that the main reason for the failure of our tactics was that we should not have split our well-trained commando unit. We divided up our best men and most daring leaders by sending twenty-seven to Bayamo, twenty-one to the hospital, and ten to the courthouse. Maybe things would have turned out differently if we had distributed our forces in some other way. The incredible coincidence of bumping into the patrol (completely accidental, since given twenty seconds either way, it would not have even been there) meant that the military camp had time to mobilize its forces; otherwise, we would have captured it without firing a shot since we already had Post 3 under our control. Another factor was that our artillery consisted almost solely of .22-caliber rifles. If we'd had hand grenades, they wouldn't have been able to resist more than fifteen minutes."

Fidel and his companions stood before the Tribunal at the Palace of Justice (the same building overrun by Raúl and his men during the Moncada attack) on Monday, September 21, 1953. A total of 122 defendants (including communists and other political prisoners) were named in what amounted to a mass trial. Because of confessions already volunteered by Fidel and his key associates, the judges were compelled from the start, by Article 148 of the Cuban constitution, to find them guilty. But the court eventually dropped charges against the political prisoners and all *Fidelistas* whose ties to the Moncada attack could not be proved.

In the beginning, Fidel appeared only as a witness. As the trial progressed, however, he used it as a forum to air his views and spread his revolutionary propaganda. His flair for oratory and sense of drama soon seized control of the proceedings. The tribunal prudently decided to bind him over for separate trial before events grew completely out of hand.

Twenty-nine rebels remained to be judged. Raúl Castro, Pedro Miret, Ernesto Tizol, and Oscar Alcalde—all part of the leadership cadre—each received thirteen years in prison. Twenty other rebels were handed ten-year sentences; three others got three-year terms. Haydée Santamaría and Melba Hernández each received seven months of detention at Guanajay, a woman's prison west of Havana. That left only Fidel.

On October 16, in exactly four hours, Fidel was tried, convicted, and sentenced to fifteen years in prison on the Isla de Pinos, the Isle of Pines. The grim island prison was modeled after the U.S. prison in Joliet, Illinois. Many who entered the prison failed to come out alive. Fidel and his Moncada attackers, however, received better treatment than regular inmates while serving their sentences. They were housed together in a special section and allowed to read, study, and talk among themselves. Fidel used the time to develop and refine his ideas for the coming revolution.

After his arrest and conviction, Fidel was sentenced to the remote Isle of Pines prison. Some prisoners were treated so badly at the prison that they failed to come out alive.

"History Will Absolve Me!"

In the courtroom of Santiago's Palace of Justice, Fidel Castro spoke for two hours in his own defense—half the time allotted to his trial. His speech, quoted in Tad Szulc's Fidel: A Critical Portrait, *rang out in patriotic eloquence, a tribute to his deep convictions, memory, and oratory skills. And it set forth the principal tenets of his revolution.*

"Fidel said, in small part: 'I bring in my heart the doctrines of Martí and in my mind the ideas of all men who have defended the freedom of the people. We have incited a rebellion against a single illegitimate power which has usurped and concentrated in its hands the legislative and executive powers of the nation. I know that I shall be silenced for many years. I know they will try to conceal the truth by every possible means. I know that there will be a conspiracy to force me into oblivion. But my voice will never be drowned; for it gathers strength within my breast when I feel most alone and it will give my heart all the warmth that cowardly souls deny me.'

To conclude his defense, Fidel said: 'I know that imprisonment will be harder for me than it ever has been for anybody, filled with threats, ruin and cowardly deeds of rage, but I do not fear it, as I do not fear the fury of the wretched tyrant who snuffed out the lives of seventy brothers of mine. Condemn me, it does not matter! *History will absolve me!*' "

"History Will Absolve Me!"

In his own defense, Fidel used two hours of his four-hour trial to deliver what has since become one of history's most prominent orations. He concluded with, "*¡Condenádme, no importa! ¡La historia me absolvera!*"—"Condemn me, it does not matter! History will absolve me!"

His now-famous speech contained precepts that were soon to become the principal tenets of his continuing revolution. His absolution still remains for history to judge.

The incident at Moncada will stay etched in military annals for all time as an absolute disaster. But politically it mothered the birth of the Cuban Revolution. "After July 26, 1953," wrote Cuban writer Guillermo Cabrera Infante, "everything in Cuba became [something] of vast historical moment—brutal, bloody, and inevitable."[19]

The long march to Havana had begun.

Chapter

2 Cuba Before the Revolution: The Long Pursuit of Freedom

When Diego de Velásquez conquered Cuba for Spain during the years 1511-15, Cubans began a four hundred-year-long pursuit of freedom. At the turn of the twentieth century, with a big assist from the United States, Cuba finally fought itself free from Spanish rule. Today, almost a century later, Cubans find themselves living at odds with their former friends to the north and in something less than freedom. The pursuit continues.

The United States started noticing Cuba not long after winning its own independence from Great Britain. Thomas Jefferson, the third U.S. president, gave much thought toward somehow acquiring the island only ninety miles south of the Florida Keys. Cuba's growing wealth would make a rich addition to the existing states. He also feared that Britain might seize Cuba from Spain and pose a threat to U.S. security. (Britain had seized Cuba in 1762, but traded the island back to Spain in return for Spain's North American colony of Florida.) But Jefferson knew that a U.S. move on Cuba would mean war with Spain. The last thing the United States needed right then was another war. Jefferson wisely held back. He held firmly to his belief, however, that acquiring Cuba would be in the best interests of the United States.

Thomas Jefferson wanted to acquire Cuba and make it part of the United States, but he didn't want to risk a conflict with Spain, who claimed the island.

Some years after leaving office, he wrote, "I candidly confess that I have ever looked on Cuba as the most interesting addition which could ever be made to our system of states."[20] As an advisor to succeeding presidents, Jefferson continued to press for a more active U.S. role in bringing Cuba into the fold. He passed along his ideas to his successor, James Madison.

Britain continued to show an interest in Cuba. In 1810, Madison received word from Albert Gallatin, an American diplomat in England, that the British were preparing to invade Cuba. Two years before, Napoleon had toppled the Spanish crown and installed his brother Joseph as head of state. Madison felt sure that Napoleon held similar designs on Cuba, as did the British. Jefferson suggested to Madison that the United States should act first and seize Cuba then. Madison, as did Jefferson before him, feared a war with Britain, and he declined the advice.

Madison settled instead for warning the European powers not to interfere in American affairs. In careful terms, he wrote, "The position of Cuba gives the United States so deep an interest in the destiny, even, of that Island, that . . . they could not be a satisfied spectator of its falling under any European government."[21] The Monroe Doctrine would echo his words, a little more forcefully, thirteen years later.

Cuba and the Monroe Doctrine

James Monroe became the fifth U.S. president in 1817 and maintained a foreign policy similar to Madison's. The now famous Monroe Doctrine grew out of a few sentences delivered by Monroe during his annual address in 1823. He pretty much repeated Madison's earlier warning to the European powers.

In part, he stated that "The American Continents . . . are henceforth not to be considered as subjects for future colonization by any European power."[22] In other words, Europe, hands off the Americas. It is worth noting that he also declared the United States' intent of staying clear of European affairs.

This doctrine established U.S. policy for years to come. As far as its effect on Cuba, it

President James Madison (left) feared that Napoleon (right), like the British, had intentions of invading Cuba. In 1810 he warned European powers not to interfere in American affairs.

President James Monroe is well known for his doctrine, which stated that the United States would not tolerate Europe becoming involved in its affairs.

the policy *la fruta madura*—the ripe fruit. To them, the U.S. position was one of preserving Cuba on the Spanish vine. When the fruit—Cuba—ripened, it would fall into the U.S. lap. Many Cubans were not prepared to wait that long. An attitude of revolt began to shape the Cuban spirit.

Between 1806 and 1823, no fewer than thirteen countries in Latin America revolted against European powers and won their freedom. The success of the "Great Liberator" Simón Bolívar in South America, the patriot-priest Miguel Hidalgo in Mexico, and others, gave rise in Cuba to a spreading desire for independence. By mid-century, Cubans extended their desire to be free of Spain to include freedom from any ties to the United States as well.

The Ten Years' War

The first war for Cuban independence began on October 10, 1868. It would last for

Simón Bolívar, the Great Liberator, led South America in a fight against European colonization.

preserved Spanish interests there for the time being. Monroe clearly would have liked to acquire Cuba, but without a fight. He held to the growing idea in the United States that Cuba would eventually become part of the Union by natural process. This idea remained constant throughout much of the nineteenth century.

Even before Monroe's time, voices in both Europe and the Americas began to speak out loudly against slave practices. In Cuba, wealthy planters welcomed the idea that the United States might soon move to bring Cuba into the Union. They didn't want to lose their slaves. By becoming a part of the United States—where some states also practiced slavery—they stood a better chance of keeping them.

After a time, however, the U.S. policy of inaction started wearing on their patience. Wealthy slaveowners who would benefit if Cuba became a U.S. state called a decade and become known as the Ten Years' War. Carlos Céspedes started the revolt at his plantation in Yara. Weary of the heavy taxes demanded by Spain, he freed his slaves and put together a mixed band of rebels.

As foreign affairs analyst Michael J. Mazarr writes:

> The movement grew rapidly under Cespedes's control. From the first group of about 150 it expanded to 4,000 by October 12, 1868; nearly 10,000 by early November; and 12,000 by the latter part of the month. On October 19 these forces captured the city of Bayamo after a number of smaller victories. Rebel units . . . were assisted by Dominican exiles, including Maximo Gomez, who had learned their tactics in the Dominican wars for independence. With this assistance, Cespedes's forces soon seized much of eastern

The Importance of the Ten Years' War

Although the rebels were defeated in their ten-year battle for independence from Spain, all was not lost. It was important for a number of reasons, as explained by analyst Michael J. Mazarr in his book Semper Fidel: America & Cuba 1776-1988.

"Though many Cubans died, thousands of others became battle-hardened veterans, instilled with a deep hatred of the Spanish and ready to fight again, as they would do a decade and a half later. Thousands of Cubans fled the island to avoid the devastation, and various Cuban independence groups sprang up in the United States and elsewhere, establishing a base of political and material support which would prove invaluable. Once slavery was abolished in Cuba, moreover, those of the Cuban planter class who opposed uprisings against the Spanish would lose their major fear—that of a slave rebellion—and many would join the ranks of those fighting for independence. The war also contributed to the growth of sentiment in the United States opposing Spanish rule and favoring Cuban independence, sentiment that would eventually contribute to the call for war at the end of the century.

Within Cuba, the period of the Ten Years' War also witnessed a further development of . . . thought that encouraged revolt against Spanish influence and would later contribute to rebellions against the American role in Cuba. Much of this thought developed in the Cuban exile communities in the United States. José Martí was its chief proponent."

Cuba, and other [rebel] groups rose up across the island.[23]

To counter the rebel uprising, Spain's Captain General Lesundi organized a group known as the *Voluntarios*, or Volunteer Corps. The corps comprised wealthy merchants, bankers, small manufacturers, and their associates. They opposed change of any sort and fought to preserve slavery.

As Mazarr writes:

> The Volunteers were civilians who supported the Spanish colonial government and who aided it by serving as garrison troops in towns and cities. This freed Spanish forces to pursue the rebels. . . . Madrid bought 90,000 Remington rifles from the United States to equip the Volunteers; thus armed they wreaked havoc and terror throughout the island.[24]

Cubans fighting for their independence would long remember that the United States supplied arms to their enemies—and nothing to them.

Ulysses S. Grant, the U.S. war hero, became president in 1868. Faced with the huge task of rebuilding the nation after the Civil War, he depended on Secretary of State Hamilton Fish to handle Cuban affairs. Fish's role in establishing Cuban policy is still hotly debated. He clearly discouraged U.S. recognition of their independence movement. What remains unclear is why.

Fish's supporters maintain that he was trying to keep the United States out of a war with Spain. The United States certainly wasn't prepared for another war at that point. In spite of this, his critics argue that he acted solely to protect U.S. business interests. Still others believe that he based his actions on someday making Cuba a state. This, of course, would not remain an option if Cuba were to win its independence. Whatever his reasons, Fish's failure to help the revolutionaries in their struggle turned many Cubans against the United States. Such feelings would simmer through long years ahead.

Motivated by such great revolutionary leaders as the generals Máximo Gómez and Calixto García, and Antonio Maceo, "The Bronze Titan," the rebels might have

The Ten Years' War was the first attempt Cubans made to be free of Spanish rule. Here, rebels are surprised by government forces.

Hamilton Fish was secretary of state immediately following the Civil War and was assigned to Cuban affairs. Fish decided that the United States should not aid Cuba's revolution.

won their fight with help from the United States. By 1875, Gómez's rebels controlled Oriente and Camagüey provinces. Gómez then launched an attack on the sugar mills of Las Villas province, destroying about one hundred mills by the torch. But time was running out on the rebels.

In the summer of 1876, Spain sent Gen. Martínez Campos to Cuba with twenty-five thousand battle-trained troops to add to the large force already there. Over the next year, the fresher, better-equipped Spaniards wore down the rebels. Although Hamilton Fish resigned in August of 1877, his Cuban policies were continued: The freedom fighters still received no help from the United States.

Finally, on May 21, 1878, the rebels agreed to the Pact of Zanjón. The pact promised certain Spanish reforms in return for a rebel surrender. After a decade of fighting, Cuba's first war for independence ended. The war was over, but the fight continued.

The "Little War"

Changes of rule in Madrid caused internal conflicts that led to Spain's failure to establish the promised reforms in Cuba. Unrest over broken promises and continued repression eventually led to Cuba's second war for independence in 1895. Several minor revolts preceded it, however, the first of which was called the "Little War." The war began on August 29, 1879, and lasted only until September 1880, hence its name. It failed badly. But it can claim importance in that it marked the first appearance of the most revered of all Cuban heroes.

José Julian Martí, "The Apostle" of Cuban liberation, began life humbly as the son of a Spanish artillery sergeant in 1853. Entering politics at age sixteen, he quickly

José Julian Martí is perhaps the most renowned Cuban liberator. Known also for his political writings, he was gunned down by the Spanish during Cuba's second war for independence.

earned fame as Cuba's poet-patriot. His political writings during the "Little War" also won him unwanted time in Spanish prisons, and eventual exile to Spain. But Martí managed an escape to New York, where he raised money and support for continued Cuban resistance.

In 1884, he met with Máximo Gómez and Antonio Maceo to plan strategy. Two more minor rebellions were easily crushed by the Spaniards in the mid-1880s. Martí then spent the next decade in the United States and Mexico. His return to Cuba would mark the beginning of Cuba's last fight to rid itself of Spanish rule.

Cuba's Second War for Independence

On April 11, 1895, along with a small band of rebels, José Martí landed at Maisí Cape on the northern coast of Cuba. Martí and his band trekked inland to link up with the rebel forces of Gen. Máximo Gómez. Ignoring Gómez's request that he move to a safe area, Martí rode off on a white horse into the Cuban brush. A not-unexpected fate awaited him there. On May 19, 1895, only thirty-nine days after his return to Cuba, the poet-patriot fell in a volley of Spanish gunfire. He became an instant martyr and a future role model for Fidel Castro.

Interestingly (because he had lived so long in the United States), Martí left a warning to his followers on the day before his death. In a letter to a friend, he wrote: "[We must] prevent in time the expansion of the United States in the Antilles, and their descending, with their additional strength, upon the lands of America. . . . I

have lived in the monster and know its insides; and my sling is that of David." [25] These words would later find a permanent home in the mind of a young man from Birán, Fidel Castro.

In December 1896, the odds of battle caught up with the man considered by many to be Cuba's greatest revolutionary leader. During a Spanish attack on his rebel camp, Antonio Maceo was shot twice. The Bronze Titan of the Ten Years' War fell dead.

The revolution of 1895 raged on. Both sides suffered huge losses in Cuba's bloodiest war ever. Once again the question was raised as to whether Cuba, with aid from the United States, might have defeated Spain by herself. The question went unanswered in light of the strange and still unexplained event of February 15, 1898.

At 9:40 P.M., the U.S. battleship *Maine* blew up in a series of explosions, killing three-quarters of the ship's crew. It began sinking at once and came to rest minutes later on the bottom of Havana harbor. Although no proof of Spanish involvement could be shown, both official and public opinion in the United States blamed the sinking on Spain. Cries of "Remember the *Maine*!" rang out across the land as Americans demanded revenge. President William McKinley heard their cries. After a century-long "hands-off" policy, the United States finally intervened in Cuba.

The United States Intervenes

In May 1898, U.S. Marines landed in Cuba and captured Guantánamo Bay in the first land action involving U.S. forces in Cuba. U.S. soldiers followed the marines ashore,

Remember the *Maine!*

The USS Maine *was a battleship of some 6,682 tons, 314 feet long, and armed with 10-inch guns, most formidable in its time. Sent to Havana by President McKinley in a "showing of the flag," its sinking plunged the United States into war with Spain. Michael J. Mazarr, in* Semper Fidel, *writes about the questionable circumstances surrounding the event.*

"As the gentle strains of taps floated out onto Havana harbor at 9:30, [Capt. Charles] Sigsbee sat quietly at his desk in the state room on the *Maine*, writing to his wife. Most of his crew had already gone to bed, and lay in their bunks throughout the ship. Suddenly, at 9:40, several explosions rocked the ship; the bow lifted out of the water and huge concussions shook its spine. Lying in shallow water, the *Maine* began to sink quickly, and soon settled on the floor of Havana bay. Two hundred sixty-six of the 354 of the sailors and marines on board perished.

For decades scholars debated the true cause of the explosion on the *Maine*. Two separate boards of inquiry concluded that the *Maine* had been sunk by an external explosion. Later evidence, however, strongly suggests that the *Maine* was destroyed by the spontaneous combustion [self-igniting] of its bituminous coal fuel—something that was a recognized phenomenon on ships of the period—which in turn ignited the ship's ammunition magazines. Certainly, the Spanish had no motive to do something that would undoubtedly provoke the United States into a military response.

In the charged atmosphere of the period, however, Spain was tried and convicted of the 'attack' of the *Maine* in both the American press and in the public mind. The demand for war became deafening."

Although the destruction of the USS Maine *is still riddled with mystery, it brought the United States into a war with Spain.*

landing at Daiquiri, east of Santiago, on June 22. This began a full-scale invasion.

The Americans, greatly superior to the Spaniards in numbers and arms, joined forces with the Cuban revolutionaries. Together, they defeated the Spaniards in only 114 days in what U.S. history books call the Spanish-American War. Cubans, however, felt (and still feel) slighted by this name—and with good reason.

Many Cubans had been fighting against the better-trained, -armed, and -equipped Spaniards for thirty years. The Americans had fought for less than four months. Of the twenty-five hundred Americans who perished during the war, most died not as a result of fighting but, rather, of disease. American sacrifices were indeed small compared with those of the Cubans. To Cubans, the war was, is, and always shall remain, Cuba's Second War of Independence.

Cubans do not believe that they owe their independence to the United States. They paid in blood and misery to free themselves from Spanish rule. Author Boris Goldenberg describes in telling words the high cost of Cuba's freedom:

> The country had been laid waste. Almost 400,000 people had died, many in big "concentration camps" into which the Spanish General [Valeriano] Weyler [who earned the nickname of "The Butcher" for his brutal acts] had collected a large part of the population. The 1899 census showed a population of 1.5 million inhabitants— 60,000 less than ten years earlier. The number of cattle had fallen by 80 per cent and tobacco production by about the same amount. The sugar harvest of 1895 had amounted to one million

tons: now it was hardly more than 300,000. The health of the population was causing anxiety for yellow fever claimed many victims. Bridges and roads had been destroyed.[26]

By whatever name history chooses to call the war of 1898, it ended in Paris at the end of that same year. Representatives from the United States and Spain met in Paris at Spain's request to reach a peace agreement. Spain did not wish to deal with Cubans directly; thus Cuba went without representation at the meeting.

The United States looked on the resulting Paris Peace Treaty of 1898 as the beginning of Cuba's independence. Cubans viewed it otherwise. Denied representation in Paris, they saw the agreement rather as an exchange of one yoke for another. Cubans resented not being allowed a voice in their own destiny.

The Americans had already shown little respect for the rights and feelings of their Cuban allies in the waning moments of the war. In Santiago, the birthplace of Cuban revolution, the Americans raised *their* flag—not Cuba's—over the governor's palace. At the same time, the Americans forcibly detained the great Cuban general Calixto García and his troops outside the city and kept them from sharing in the victory. This unfeeling display of American arrogance did little to foster Cuban goodwill.

The Platt Amendment

The United States further lessened its popularity among Cubans by enacting the Platt Amendment of 1901. The amend-

The Battle of San Juan Hill

Except for the officers, the famous Rough Riders—under Col. Teddy Roosevelt—charged San Juan Hill outside Santiago on foot. According to a quote from Michael J. Mazarr's Semper Fidel, *Roosevelt later recalled:*

"Being on horseback I was, of course, able to get ahead of my men on foot, excepting my orderly, Henry Bardshar, who had run ahead very fast in order to get better shots at the Spaniards, who were now running out of the ranch buildings. . . . Some forty yards from the top I ran into a wire fence and jumped off Little Texas [his horse], turning him loose. . . . As I ran up the hill, Bardshar stopped to shoot, and two Spaniards fell as he emptied his magazine. These were the only Spaniards I actually saw fall to aimed shots by any of my men, with the exception of two guerrillas in trees."

Teddy Roosevelt and his Rough Riders led the attack on San Juan Hill during the Spanish-American War.

ment stated, in effect, that the United States had the right to intervene in Cuba whenever her interests demanded it. In practice, this amounted to making Cuba an economic colony of the United States for the next fifty years. To many Cubans, their years of struggle resulted only in shifting control of their lives from Spain to the United States. True independence remained only a voice that whispered to the Cuban soul.

With the founding of the Republic of Cuba in 1902, Cubans shifted their struggle for freedom from the battlefield to the political arena. The first third of the new century proved to be a period of trial and error, consent and dissent. Unused to self-government, Cuba became prey to a pa-

In spite of the fact that it was supposed to establish Cuba's independence, the Paris Peace Treaty was signed with no Cuban representation (left). The United States, indeed, did not seem to have Cuba's independence as its prime goal after the war. After defeating the Spanish, Americans raise their flag, not Cuba's, in Santiago (below).

rade of self-serving profit seekers. As journalist and author Herbert L. Matthews writes:

> Politics, from the beginning of the Republic, was a spoils system, a profession, a means of enriching oneself and one's family, and of gaining . . . social prestige in the process. There were honorable exceptions, of course, but the rule was that politicians, high army officers, bankers, businessmen and landowners served themselves and their families and not their country and their people.[27]

The U.S. role in Cuban affairs during this period, however well meaning, cannot escape some criticism. As Matthews goes on:

> The United States supported their system because it protected American property; permitted generations of Americans to make money in or from Cuba; provided friendly Cuban governments in a country of the highest strategic value to the United States; and, finally, ensured a crude sort of stability and order.[28]

The United States acted twice in Cuba under the terms of the Platt Amendment,

the first time at the request of Tomás Estrada Palma, Cuba's first president. Estrada Palma, who feared an armed revolt by liberals who opposed his government, suspended the Cuban Constitution and called for U.S. help on September 10, 1906.

The United States responded and set up a temporary government in Havana, headed at first by U.S. secretary of war

Howard Taft. Taft gave way to U.S. lawyer Charles Magoon on October 13, 1906. Magoon served as American provisional governor for twenty-eight months. Under Magoon, the United States restored and maintained order in Cuba.

In 1917, U.S.-owned sugar mills came under threat of attack by Liberal Party members who wanted to rid Cuba of U.S. interests. The United States sent two thousand marines from Guantánamo Bay to Camagüey province to guard the threatened sugar mills. This act concluded U.S. *physical* intervention in Cuba. (It should be stated that the naval base at Guantánamo Bay was established by right of the Platt Amendment and later by treaty with the Cubans. Under terms of the treaty, the base is still leased by the United States for an annual fee of four thousand dollars. Fidel Castro maintains that the treaty is not valid but has never interfered with U.S. operations in Guantánamo.)

Gen. Gerardo Machado y Morales, Cuba's fifth president, became increasingly dictatorial. By his second term, he used the military to enforce political arrests, torture, and killings.

First Cuban president Tomás Estrada Palma asked for U.S. intervention to help him put down revolts against the government. The U.S. responded by setting up a provisional government in Cuba.

U.S. political and financial influence continued for much longer. Such influence went a long way in stripping a succession of Cuban governments of any real power. Cuban politicians found themselves with little to do. In the absence of true personal authority, they busily engaged themselves in corruption and graft. The government of Gerardo Machado excelled in these activities.

The First Dictator

Gen. Gerardo Machado y Morales became Cuba's fifth president in 1924. Machado could serve as a pattern for the typical Latin American dictator. After a quiet and fairly decent first term, his second term

As Machado lost his grip on the military, he lost his power, and was eventually overthrown in the Revolution of 1933.

sank to new lows of government rule by force. He presided over censorship, political arrests, torture, killings, and other cruelties, so as to remain in office.

Machado's rule embraced all the elements that inspire revolutions. Labor leaders who opposed him became targets for assassins. After a visit to Cuba in 1927, William Green, president of the American Federation of Labor, said that "a condition of virtual terrorism existed."[29] That condition lasted for six more years.

The Revolution of 1933

The Revolution of 1933 erupted in a series of small uprisings rather than in one great revolt. While supported by the army, Machado kept control of government. But the ever-increasing discontent and growing acts of violence across Cuba convinced the army to back off. On August 12, 1933, Machado, while he still had the chance, fled Cuba for the Bahamas.

Directed by the hand of U.S. influence, Carlos Manuel de Céspedes, Cuba's ambassador to Mexico, succeeded Machado as president. The U.S. choice of Céspedes proved unacceptable to the noncommissioned officers of the Cuban army. On September 4, in a unified action known as "The Revolt of the Sergeants," they seized control of all the army based in Cuba. Thereafter, they demanded a role in government and certain other accommodations.

The United States stepped in to bargain with a five-person group called the "Pentarchy," set up by the sergeants to represent them. A sergeant named Fulgencio Batista emerged as leader of the group. By September 9, all parties agreed to install Dr. Ramón Grau San Martín as Cuba's seventh president. But the newly appointed Colonel Batista retained *de facto* (actual) control of government.

In 1940, Batista ran for president on his own, was elected, and served one mildly successful term in office. Grau San Martín then returned to office for another four years, followed by Carlos Prío Socarrás. Prío's term lasted until Batista decided to become president again on March 10, 1952.

Batista's unlawful seizure of power opened the door to the Cuban Revolution. And Fidel Castro stood on the threshold.

3 Castro: Man of Destiny

An air of mystery seems to surround everything that Fidel Castro does. For forty years, he has held Cuba and the world in a continuing state of second-guessing. Even the date of his birth remains subject to question. He entered the world at ten pounds, a Leo, born at 2:00 A.M. on August 13. His sisters insist that he was born in 1927. Fidel's parents claim that he was born in 1926. Fidel agrees with his parents and maintains that it was 1926, although willing to accept a year off his age. When asked about it, he said, "I would have been an even younger chief of government, thirty-one years old and not thirty-two, when we won the Revolution."[30] It seems unlikely that Fidel would miss a chance to show achievement at an even younger age.

A man of supreme ego, he appears to have an almost mystic regard for his place in history. Even the hour of his birth cry assumes special meaning when seen through a veil of grand ambition: "I was born a *guerrillero*, because I was born at night, around two o'clock of the dawn," he once told Frei Betto, a Dominican friar. "It seems that night might have had an influence in my *guerrilla* spirit, in the revolutionary activity."[31] Fidel apparently believed that his nighttime birth linked him to the hours of darkness, which are best suited to guerrilla activities.

Whether born or fashioned to greatness or lesser station, Fidel drew his first breath on his father's sugar plantation near Birán. He entered the world in which he was to become an international figure as the son of unwed parents. Fidel rarely speaks of it, but he does recall that other children called him "the Jew" during his boyhood. He didn't know why at the time, but he guessed that it had something to do with his not having been christened. That would come later. In the meantime, he often suffered the sting of unkind words from his peers.

Fidel's Roots

Fidel's father, Angel María Bautista Castro Arguiz, had immigrated to Cuba from Galicia, Spain's northernmost province. His Creole mother, Lina Ruz González, came from Pinar del Río at the far western end of Cuba. She joined the Castro household as a live-in maid and stayed on. Her family also came from Galicia. A more famous Galician was to become an early role model for Fidel: Spain's mighty *caudillo* (leader) Generalisimo Francisco Franco. Fidel has always found great pride in claiming his *Gallego* (a person born in Galicia) roots.

Fidel's father came from Galicia, a Spanish province, where Francisco Franco (above), Spain's leader, was also born. Fidel saw the connection as significant.

In Galicia, an area once ruled by the Celts and fought over by Roman legions, people grew hard to match the hard land. The northernmost province of Spain, Galicia's high cliffs face the sea defiantly, lashed continually by winds and storms. Its unfertile and barren land makes merely living a challenge to even the very strong. Houses stand half-finished and deserted by those who left in order to survive. Many Gallegos welcomed the war of 1898 and the chance to go to the New World. Spain's fight in Cuba offered them a limited escape from a life of endless toil and poverty. After the war, Angel Castro elected to remain in Cuba and carve out a future for himself and his family in the wilds of Oriente province.

Angel Castro worked hard—at one point selling lemonade to field-workers— and saved his money. During this time, he learned how to read and write. He began buying sections of land from the United States-owned United Fruit Company. Soon, he employed workers—mostly Hait-ian—to work the land and harvest sugar-cane. He sold the cane back to the United Fruit Company and bought more land. Then he bought a lumber mill and sold railroad ties to the Americans. Next he opened a general store in Birán and be-gan selling cattle. Step by step, he became a wealthy landowner and earned the title of *Don* Angel Castro. In 1910, he turned thirty-five and married María Louisa Ar-gota, a Cuban schoolteacher.

Angel fathered two children with María Argota—Pedro Emilio and Lidia—before becoming attracted to Lina. Together, An-gel and Lina produced seven more chil-dren. The first three—Angela, Ramón, and Fidel—were born while Angel was still mar-ried to María Argota. It remains unclear as to what happened to María. Some accounts indicate that Angel divorced her, others say that she died; still others hint that she just left Angel, never to be heard from again. In any case, Angel eventually married Lina, if only to enable their children's admittance to Catholic schools.

Galicia is a barren area full of wind-blown cliffs. Only a few people manage to carve out a meager existence in this environment. Fidel thought his will to survive and fight came from the Galician stock of his father.

Lina then took charge of the Castro household at Las Manacas, Angel's twenty-six-thousand-acre estate or *finca*. The main, two-story house was built on stilts and modeled after the homes of wealthy Galicians. Angel added on to it as required by the needs of a growing family. The space beneath the house served as a barn for cattle and fowl. Chickens pecked and perched around the living quarters at will. Lina, far from being a neat house-keeper, didn't seem to mind.

Nor did her son Fidel, who told Carlos Franqui:

Castro with his mother, Lina. Lina bore Castro while working as a maid in his father's house.

> I was born into a family of landowners in comfortable circumstances. We were considered rich and treated as such. I was brought up with all the privileges attendant to a son in such a family. Everyone lavished attention on me, flattered me, and treated me differently from the other boys we played with when we were children. These other children went barefoot while we wore shoes; they were often hungry; at our house, there was always a squabble at table to get us to eat."[32]

The Castros gathered in their large kitchen for a family meal once every day. Lina called them together by firing off a shotgun. They ate standing up. Other than their hands, they used only a sharp knife. Fidel carried these eating habits into his later years. As historian and biographer Professor Robert E. Quirk writes:

> All his life Fidel Castro preferred to eat foods that could be held in the hands and attacked—especially barbecued pork and fried chicken. Often in Havana, when the revolution had taken power, he would turn up late at night in the kitchen of a hotel or restaurant to eat, standing up, and talk through the night with the workers. He felt more comfortable with them than in the great world of politics.[33]

Even though Fidel felt "privileged" as a boy, he appears never to have looked down on those less fortunate than he. He recalled that "one circumstance in the middle of all this helped us develop a certain human spirit: it was the fact that all our friends, our companions, were the sons of local peasants."[34] Once he started school, however, his "human spirit" often veered from its earlier humble aspect.

Early School Days

Fidel began school at the age of four in the public grammar school in Marcané. Of his conduct there, Fidel said:

> I spent most of my time being fresh in school. Maybe because of my family's

position, or my age, I remember that whenever I disagreed with something that teacher said to me, or whenever I got mad, I would swear at her and immediately leave school, running as fast as I could. There was a kind of standing war between us [the students] and the teacher.[35]

Between battles, however, he somehow learned to read and write before he was five years old.

In 1932, Fidel's parents finally decided to send Fidel and his older sister Angela to Catholic schools in Santiago. Fidel attended the La Salle school, run by the Marist brothers, while Angela went to a girls' school. They shared the unhappy experience of boarding with their godparents in Santiago. Fidel isn't sure whether he was sent away "because I caused too much trouble at home, or because my teacher convinced my family that it would be a good idea to send me away to school." His exact age at the time escapes him, but he does recall "that I wet the bed on the first night."[36]

Perhaps the happiest days of his life came when school let out that year. Fidel remembered, "On our first holidays, we went home for a three-month vacation; I don't think I've ever been happier. We hunted with slingshots, rode horseback, swam in the rivers, and had complete freedom during those months."[37]

Later, his brothers Ramón and Raúl joined him at La Salle school. Together, they established themselves as "the three biggest bullies that had ever gone there."[38] Angel decided in 1935 that the three of them had had enough schooling. But even then Fidel recognized the value of an education and rebelled.

"I remember going to my mother and explaining that I wanted to go on studying; it wasn't fair not to let me go to school. I appealed to her and told her . . . that if I wasn't sent back, I'd set fire to the house."[39] They thought it best to honor his wish. From his exercise in minor blackmail, Fidel learned the value of being bold and stubborn. He would not forget.

Jesuit Training

Fidel's Jesuit education began at the age of nine. On his return to Santiago, he entered Colegio Dolores. It was a better but more difficult school than La Salle. Never a good student, he succeeded in getting passing grades mostly on the strength of his excellent memory. He would cram on the night before a test and memorize the study material almost word for word.

His favorite subjects, especially history and geography, he remembered without cramming. He loved to read about Cuba's great freedom fighters and their struggles for independence against Spain. Tales of José Martí, Máximo Gómez, Antonio Maceo, Calixto García—all the great ones—set his imagination to flight. Accounts of ancient battles would hold his attention for hours. He even felt a certain kinship with Alexander the Great because Fidel's middle name was Alejandro. And already he had fought some battles of his own.

His brother Raúl enjoys speaking of Fidel's schoolboy encounters. "Every day he would fight. He had a very explosive character. He challenged the biggest and the strongest ones, and when he was beaten, he started it all over again the next day. He would never quit."[40] It seemed as if he were always testing himself, preparing his mind, his will, his body for a greater test to come.

Fidel's love affair with the mountains began during his last year at Dolores. He told Carlos Franqui:

> We would go on outings in a school. We'd arrive at El Cobre and often I would decide to climb the mountain, keeping the bus waiting for two or three hours. Or we would go somewhere near El Caney, and I'd also go climb the tallest hill there. . . . The bus always had to wait for me. . . . I did not imagine that mountains would one day play such an important role in my life.[41]

Fidel would later live and fight in the Sierra Maestra of Oriente province for twenty-five months.

Fidel carried his fondness for mountain climbing into the next important phase of his life as a student. Two months after his sixteenth birthday, he moved to Havana with his sister Angela. Now eighteen, Angela looked after him while he attended the highly regarded Colegio Belén, another Jesuit school. He took an active interest in sports and was soon named head of the school's hiking team. More to his credit, when he failed to make the basketball team, he refused to quit. Instead, he kept practicing until he made the team and was chosen as its captain in his senior year. He also played baseball, insisting always on pitching. But he never learned how to control his fastball.

Belén represented a giant step for young Fidel. It marked the first time that he had ventured from the familiar and friendly surroundings of Oriente province. And he began to realize the importance of his Jesuit training. The brothers had

Fidel excelled at the Jesuit college, Colegio Belén. He was named best athlete in the school in 1945, the honor for which this yearbook photo was taken.

taught him the value of self-esteem and a sense of justice. Beyond all else, Belén opened the door to the university. When he graduated in 1945, the school yearbook described him with remarkable vision:

> 1942-1945. Fidel distinguished himself always in all subjects related to letters. His record was one of excellence, he was a true athlete, always defending with bravery and pride the flag of the school. He has known how to win the admiration and the affection of all. He will make law his career and we do not doubt that he will fill with brilliant pages the book of his life. He has good timber and the actor in him will not be lacking.[42]

Shortly before graduating from Belén, Fidel climbed the highest mountain in Pinar del Río. The view from the summit of Pan de Guajaibón—a view from the top—was one that he would become used to in the years ahead. Soon, he would enter the University of Havana. There, he would study for the profession of law—but he would learn the politics of revolution.

At the University of Havana

Until this time, Fidel's ability as an athlete had kept him at the center of attention, a student leader. But the University of Havana didn't support organized sports. He would have to seek another way to stay ahead of the pack. An active role in politics offered the only available outlet for his natural urge to lead. Without bothering to test the waters, he plunged right into a pool of political strife and struggle. The year was 1945 and he had just turned nineteen years old.

At the university's Faculty of Law, Fidel took to the political waters like a world-class swimmer at the Olympics. Of his early days on campus, he later said:

> At the university, I had the feeling that a new field was opening up for me. I started thinking of my country's political problems—almost without being conscious of it. I . . . started to feel a certain concern, an interest in social and political questions.[43]

To Fidel, feeling an interest in something meant becoming totally involved and committed to it.

He set his sights on becoming president of the powerful *Federación Estudiantil Universitaria* (FEU, University Students' Federation). Membership in the union at that time represented a major step up on the stairway to national political power.

His attempt to become president of the FEU failed by a wide margin, probably because he wasn't enough of a team player. Although he never managed to win election to any high office in the FEU, he remained politically active.

The two most important political groups at the time—both on and off campus—were the Socialist Revolutionary Movement (MSR) and the Insurrectional Revolutionary Union (UIR). Fidel courted the favors of both, while keeping a high profile and developing his own fiery brand of politics.

By law, the university governed and policed itself. Neither the police nor the army was allowed on campus. It therefore stood as an island refuge for the practice of violent politics. Known gangsters, as well as students, roamed the campus freely in armed support of their differing aims and causes. Personal danger came in company with taking part in campus politics. Fidel

Because the University of Havana did not sponsor sports, Fidel (pictured in his university yearbook photo) became heavily involved in politics.

A quote from Tad Szulc's biography of Castro reveals Fidel's thoughts when he was warned to stop his criticism of the government or else leave the university.

"This was the moment of great decision. The conflict hit me like a cyclone. Alone, on the beach, facing the sea, I examined the situation. If I returned to the university, I would face personal danger, physical risk. . . . But not to return would be to give in to the threats, to admit my defeat by some killer, to abandon my own ideals and aspirations. I decided to return, and I returned—armed."

took to carrying a .45-caliber pistol almost everywhere he went. It became only a matter of time before he would use it.

In December of 1945, Fidel shot and wounded Leonel Gómez, president of the Students' Federation at the Havana High School and prominent member of a UIR gang. It is worth noting that student rivals at that time often settled their differences with guns. Fidel's motive in the shooting was to win approval from rival gang leader Manolo Castro (no relation) of the MSR. Fidel held hopes of taking Manolo's place in the MSR after first gaining the gang leader's confidence. But he failed to impress Manolo, who instead later became his enemy. Oddly, he did gain favor with Emílio Tro, head of the UIR, Leonel Gómez's own gang.

According to Fidel's friend Max Lesnick, "It seemed that Emílio Tro had a certain sympathy for Fidel and, far from acting on the consequences of the aggression suffered by one of his men, Tro was converted into a *padrino* or godfather of Fidel."[44] Fidel was then welcomed into the UIR. Charges were never brought against

him for the shooting, and the event was soon forgotten.

Nor was this the only shooting involving Fidel. A fellow student accused him of shooting (and killing) a police sergeant two years later. But authorities dropped charges against Fidel when the supposed witness withdrew his story.

The Cayo Confites Expedition

In the summer of 1947, always alert to ways of furthering his revolutionary image, Fidel joined in an ill-fated attempt to invade the Dominican Republic. The Cayo Confites Expedition, named after its Cuban point of origin, was directed by the Dominican patriot Juan Bosch. He and his Cuban sympathizers hoped to overthrow the government of dictator Rafael Leónidas Trujillo.

When Angel Castro learned of his son's involvement in the flighty affair, he offered Fidel an automobile to stay out of it. But Fidel felt a higher calling. He told his father dramatically:

> You don't seem to realize, Papa, that Cuba was liberated through the great efforts of a Dominican, General Máximo Gómez. And that we Cubans have a debt of honor with Santo Domingo. I want to pay this debt, and it is because of this that I want to fight against Trujillo.[45]

Three ships left out of Cayo Confites, one of them bearing Fidel, only to be ordered back by President Grau San Martín. To avoid arrest, Fidel, carrying a submachine gun, jumped off the ship. Across the shark-filled waters of the Bay of Nipe, he swam nine miles to shore—while holding the gun above his head. Truly the stuff that shapes legends. Once begun, the legend continued to grow, aided largely by Fidel's own ability to inspire myth.

The Ninth International Conference of American States was scheduled to meet in Bogotá, the capital of Colombia, in early April of 1948. Representatives from Western Hemisphere nations met annually to discuss ways for improving life in the Americas. The objective of this year's meeting was to create the Organization of American States (OAS)—the regional organization of the United Nations. No less a figure than George C. Marshall—the great World War II general and then secretary of state—would represent the United States.

The *Bogotazo*

Fidel was by then convinced that the United States acted solely in its own best interests. Always the student of José Martí,

In one of his first revolutionary attempts, Fidel participated in a failed coup to oust Dominican Republic dictator Rafael Leónidas Trujillo.

he was equally certain that U.S. interests didn't serve those of Cuba and the rest of Latin America. So, unsurprisingly, he and other political activists organized a student conference to protest against the United States during the Conference of American States in Bogotá. The events that followed became known as the *Bogotazo*, which might best be defined as a wild riot scene in Bogotá. The riot resulted in the deaths of about three thousand people.

On March 31, 1948, Fidel and three other Cuban students arrived in Bogotá. Argentina's dictator, Juan Perón—who had sent an agent to Cuba to recruit protestors—paid for their trip in trade for their support of his own anti-American efforts. Fidel quickly arranged a meeting with Jorge Eliecer Gaitán, the popular leader of Colombia's Liberal Party. Rafael del Pino joined Fidel and they met Gaitán on April 7 in his downtown law office. Fidel said later that Gaitán "grew very enthused about the idea of the congress [student conference], and he offered us his support. He conversed with us, and he was totally in agreement with the idea of closing the congress with a great mass demonstration."[46] Gaitán invited the two students to meet with him again on April 9, whereupon Fidel and Rafael left.

On April 9, about three hours before his scheduled meeting with the two Cubans, Gaitán stepped out of his office building. Moments later he lay dead in a pool of his own blood, shot several times by a madman named Juan Roa. Reports differ, but Roa was either hanged or beaten to death on the spot by a mob. News of the shooting spread rapidly throughout the city, setting off several days of rioting, looting, and burning.

Fidel remembers the scene clearly:

I was in the middle of the park, where I could see what was happening. People were wrecking streetlights; rocks

Jorge Eliecer Gaitán, the leader of Colombia's Liberal Party, was brutally assassinated, leading to massive riots in Bogotá.

Argentina's dictator Juan Perón paid for Castro's trip to Bogotá in order to prompt anti-American protests there.

flew in all directions. Meanwhile, someone was trying to speak from a balcony, but no one listened or could have. Glass store fronts were shattering, and it was impossible to tell what would happen next, but a popular uprising was obviously under way.[47]

False rumors and half-truths arose from the Colombian chaos to cloud the details of Fidel's part in the events that followed. Claims that linked him to several shootings and a radio broadcast announcing a communist revolution appear to be untrue. Nor was Fidel in any other way working for the communists at that time. The whole truth will perhaps never be known. From what *is* known, it seems likely that Fidel played no more than a minor role in the affair. But just his *being* there added enormously to his growing legend. Despite the wild environment, the Ninth International Conference of Ameri-

Twentieth-Century Knight-Errant

While at the University of Havana, Fidel Castro saw what he believed to be many wrongs in the world that needed righting. Carlos Franqui wrote in his Diary of the Cuban Revolution *that Fidel later told him:*

"In those days I was quixotic [foolishly impractical in pursuit of ideals], romantic, a dreamer, with very little political know-how but with a tremendous thirst for knowledge and a great impatience for action. . . . The dreams of Martí and Bolívar, as well as a kind of [ideal] socialism, were vaguely stirring within me. . . . Democracy was still a magic word for us. In its name, the blood of millions had been spilled on battlefields in a war we read about with the passionate interest boys can show for historical as well as current events. . . . As a matter of fact, we were ready to give our lives for that democracy."

Three thousand people died in the Bogotá riots that followed Gaitán's assassination in 1948.

can States persisted with its business. The Organization of American States was founded on April 30, 1948.

With the help of the Cuban consul, Fidel flew back to Cuba on a plane carrying bulls to Havana for a bullfight. Fidel would not forget the lessons of Bogotá:

> Thousands of people from the poorest neighborhoods on the outskirts of Bogotá had started looting. . . . This unfortunate sight was an important lesson for me; later, during our Revolution, I constantly reminded Cubans not to do anything like that, even though I was sure looting could never happen in our case, with our people being more politically advanced than these.[48]

Fidel saved experiences as some people save money, always looking for ways to invest them in the future.

On his return from Bogotá, Fidel experienced romantic love for the first time. He met Mirta Díaz-Balart in the law school

Castro married Mirta Díaz-Balart in 1948. In 1949, she bore him a son, Fidelito.

named after the father in the Cuban way. For a time, they were happy. But Fidel's enthusiasm over his new son soon wore off, as did his earlier zeal for Mirta.

Fidel began to lose himself in his political activities outside the home to the near-total neglect of his wife and son. Perhaps some people are not meant to marry. Fidel, much the same as his idol José Martí, was one of these people. Of their similar traits, Tad Szulc wrote: "Both were married at a very young age, and Martí never could spare time for his wife and family. Castro, as it would turn out, had no time for his family either—despite his great emotional attachment to his son."[49] The marriage dissolved after five years while Fidel was confined in prison on the Isle of Pines. He would never marry again.

Destiny Beckons

In September of 1950, Fidel graduated from the University of Havana with three degrees: Doctors of Law, Social Sciences, and Diplomatic Law. He opened a law office in Havana but practiced little. Again, his politics came first. Attracted to the political views of Senator Eduardo Chibás, leader of the *Ortodoxo* Party, Fidel worked hard to prevent the reelection of President Prío Socarrás. Through the press and broadcast media, he railed against the Prío government. Finally, he declared himself a candidate for congress in the 1952 elections. But Batista's coup on March 10 left Fidel a candidate with no election in sight. At the same time, however, it established a climate for revolution.

And a young Gallego from Birán drew nearer to his destiny.

cafeteria; she was introduced to him by her brother Rafael. Her lime-colored eyes and rose-tinted lips, set in a frame of golden hair, turned his head and seized his heart. And Fidel, of the classic profile, curly brown hair, and brooding eyes, won her love on the instant. They pledged themselves to one another that fall, taking their wedding vows on October 10, 1948.

Interestingly, Carlos Prío Socarrás succeeded Ramón Grau San Martín as Cuba's president on that same day. Even on his wedding day, Fidel kept a watchful eye on the man whose administration he would soon work against.

Mirta's wealthy father presented the young couple with ten thousand dollars for a three-month honeymoon in—of all places—the United States. They spent some time in Miami, then traveled on to New York, before returning to set up housekeeping in Havana. On September 1, 1949, Mirta bore Fidel's only son Fidelito,

4 M-26 in Mexico: The Preparation

On May 15, 1955, Fidel Castro, his brother Raúl, and other members of the M-26 (26th of July Movement), were released from prison on the Isle of Pines. Members of the opposing *Ortodoxo* Party had appealed for the release of Fidel and other Moncada prisoners. The newly reelected and confident Batista figured wrongly that the *Fidelistas* no longer threatened his regime and agreed to grant them amnesty. In exchange for the amnesty, the *Ortodoxos* surrendered several of their seats in the Cuban senate to loyal Batista supporters.

Shortly after his release, Fidel announced to the press that he would leave Cuba. "The peaceful struggle is over," he told reporters.[50] They could only wonder what he meant.

Fidel left for Mexico on July 7, leaving behind a message that was published in twenty-five thousand copies of Cuba's leading magazine *Bohemia:*

> I am leaving Cuba because all doors of peaceful struggle have been closed to me. Six weeks after being released from prison I am convinced more than ever of the dictatorship's intention to remain in power . . . ignoring the patience of the Cuban people, which has its limits. As a follower of Martí, I believe the hour has come to take rights and not to beg for them, to

fight instead of pleading for them. I will reside somewhere in the Caribbean. From trips such as this, one does not return or else one returns with the tyranny beheaded at one's feet.[51]

Fidel and a small core of followers would spend the next sixteen months in and around Mexico City, preparing to free Cuba or die trying. Another small group of about twenty people remained behind, prepared by Fidel to continue the movement's work on the island.

Those left behind included Haydée Santamaría, Pedro Miret, and Lester Rodríguez, old comrades from Moncada. Numbered among the more recent members of the movement were Frank País and Pepito Tey, leaders of the Santiago students; Faustino Pérez, a chemist; Armando Hart, a law student; and Enrique Oltuski, son of a Polish immigrant. Another notable member of this group was ex-communist Carlos Franqui, an old acquaintance of Fidel's from the Cayo Confites Expedition. A journalist for the magazine *Carteles*, Franqui would organize the mimeographed paper *Revolución*. He would later become the diarist of the Cuban Revolution.

These people, then, became the principal organizers of the 26th of July Movement within Cuba. Earlier, Frank País, son of the pastor of Santiago's First Baptist Church, had put together his own movement called the *Acción Revolucionaria Oriente* (ANR). Because of País's experience, Fidel named him as head of all "action groups" in Cuba.

Guerrilla General

In Mexico City, Fidel approached Alberto Bayo right away for help in training his *guerrilleros*. The Cuban-born Bayo had served as a Republican general in the fight against Francisco Franco in Spain's civil war. Before that, he had served *under* Franco in North Africa, commanding a guerrilla force against the Moors for eleven years. He lost an eye in the process. Fidel had read several of the general's books on guerrilla warfare and recognized Bayo's potential value to the movement. Then the owner of a furniture factory in

While staying in Mexico City and organizing his revolutionaries, Castro asked Alberto Bayo to train his troops in guerrilla tactics.

In 1955, Castro toured the United States to solicit funds from Cuban exiles for his revolutionary movement. He raised thousands of dollars on this tour, which included New York, where this photo was taken.

Mexico, Bayo had become a fighter without a fray. He agreed to help Fidel, but not without some serious misgivings.

In his later book about training the *Fidelistas*, he told of his first meeting with Fidel:

> The young man was telling me that he expected to defeat Batista in a future landing that he planned to carry out with men "when I have them," and with vessels "when I have the money to buy them," because at the moment he was talking to me, he had neither a man nor a dollar. . . . Wasn't it amusing? Wasn't it child's play? . . . Come now, I thought, this young man wants to move mountains with one hand. But what did it cost me to please him? "Yes," I said. . . . We shook hands, and all this seemed impossible to me.[52]

In October 1955, Fidel left on a tour of the United States to raise money for the revolution, visiting New York, Philadelphia, and Miami. Much like "The Apostle"

José Martí before him, Fidel held meetings among Cuban exiles who opposed the current regime in Cuba. Conducting his affairs openly, he attracted little attention outside the Cuban community. Although he was watched closely and questioned by FBI agents and police detectives in New York, he was never taken into custody. He made many speeches and collected thousands of dollars from the exiles. When he returned seven weeks later, training began in earnest.

In an article prepared for *Cuba Socialista* ten years later, Faustino Pérez described the training this way:

> The time was short and an intensive program of training was prepared. The conditions were purposely made hard so that no one would be unprepared for what he was going to face in Cuba—shooting practice, marches, maneuvers, river crossings, mountain climbing, long marches in silence, living in the open, [simple] food, and, along with all that, the spiny cactuses and the rattlesnakes constantly waiting in ambush.[53]

Most of the training took place about twenty-five miles outside Mexico City. Alberto Bayo had rented a ranch called Santa Rosa, located near the town of Chalco. Spread over ninety-five square miles of rugged, arid country, the ranch provided an ideal training site. Bayo, the tough old guerrilla leader, ran his charges from sunup to sundown. He added night marches commencing at 8:00 P.M. toward the end of their training. At one point, the crusty general told them, "Very few of you will survive in Cuba; you are going to win, but from you there will remain few."[54] His prediction held up.

Fidel kept himself apart from the training, attending to the more pressing demands of planning the expedition in Mexico City. Conversely, a young doctor from Córdoba, Argentina, was very involved in the training. The Argentine was quickly gaining recognition as Bayo's most apt student. His name was Ernesto "Che" Guevara.

Beyond dispute, the mysterious, dashing figure of Che stood taller than any other of Fidel's followers. Few accounts of the man's life exist that don't include the word *legend* when describing him. His name has become one with the Cuban Revolution, second only to that of Fidel himself. The two legends met one night in early July of 1955 in Mexico City. Behind iron gates in the stucco home of Cuban exile María Antonia González, they talked for ten straight hours. Their similar but different personalities blended like *arroz con pollo*—rice with chicken, a much-liked Cuban dish.

Che Guevara (right) was a young physician when he became involved in Castro's revolutionary movement. It was Guevara's political leanings that exposed Castro to communism.

Che later wrote: "At dawn, I was already the physician of the future expedition." Still later, he wrote that he had been "moved by a feeling of romantic adventurous sympathy, and by the conviction that it would be worth dying on an alien beach for such a pure idea [as Fidel's revolution]."[55]

Of the two men, Che's wife Hilda later said, "Without Ernesto Guevara, Fidel Castro might never have become a Communist. Without Fidel Castro, Ernesto Guevara might never have become more than a Marxist theorist, an intellectual idealist."[56]

At the time of their meeting, neither Che nor Fidel had adopted communism, although Che's thinking leaned sharply in that direction. Without doubt, Che's views strongly affected those of Fidel. Although primarily a man of ideas and ideals, Che would demonstrate in the months ahead that he was also a man of action.

Raúl Castro was another important person in Castro's revolution. Eager and competent, he became fast friends with Che Guevara, sharing Guevara's enthusiasm for communism.

Bonded in Brotherhood

Raúl Castro, Fidel's younger brother and always faithful supporter, was another man of action. Raúl had arrived in Mexico on June 24, two weeks in advance of most other *Fidelistas*, to prepare the way. Raúl met Che and the pair became fast friends at once. They began meeting every day.

Hilda Guevara later recalled that Raúl had communist ideas and admired the Soviet Union. She said that he "believed that the struggle for power was to make a revolution on behalf of the people, and that this struggle was not only for the people of Cuba, but for Latin America and against Yankee imperialism." She added that "it was stimulating for the spirit to talk with Raúl: He was merry, open, sure of himself, very clear in [explaining] his ideas [and in breaking them down to show how all parts worked together]. This is why he got along so well with Ernesto."[57]

Raúl enjoyed a special one-of-a-kind kinship with Fidel, quite beyond the ordinary brotherly regard for one another. In school, at Moncada, and now in Mexico, Raúl stood loyally and ably at Fidel's right hand. He would remain there throughout the stormy years ahead and into the present day. His fierce loyalty would find its reward down the road when the struggle ended in success: Fidel would eventually name his brother and chief lieutenant heir to the Cuban head of state and government.

As of this writing, Raúl still serves his brother as first vice president of both the Council of State and the Council of Minis-

Portrait of a Leader

Teresa Casuso, a Cuban exile, visited Fidel in a Mexican prison. In her book Cuba and Castro, *she describes him as he seemed to her during that difficult time in his life:*

"Tall and clean-shaven, and with close-cropped chestnut hair, dressed soberly and correctly . . . standing out from the rest by his look and bearing. He gave one the impression of being noble, sure, deliberate . . . eminently serene. His voice was quiet, his expression grave, his manner calm, gentle.

Fidel showed that he had read a great deal of José Martí who seemed indeed to be the guiding spirit of his life.

The plans he revealed seemed beyond his reach and I felt a kind of pity for this aspiring deliverer who was so full of confidence and firm conviction and I was moved by his innocence [yet] I could not give myself up to the intense admiration which he inspired in his group of young men. Fidel and his young men seemed to me to be a lost cause."

ters. He also serves as second secretary of the Communist Party and defense minister, and holds the title of General of the Army. Raúl's position as the second most powerful person in Cuba assures his succession, but only if Fidel should die in office or elect to retire as Cuba's leader.

The aches and agonies of guerrilla training under Bayo continued, interrupted all too often now by the Mexican police. Inspired by Mexico's Foreign Ministry, which didn't approve of revolutionary activities, the police arrested a number of M-26 members and seized their weapons. Fidel himself was arrested at one point but was soon released. Repeated problems with the police finally forced the rebels out of their Santa Rosa training site. With time growing short, they set up final training camps in Jalapa, Tamaulipas, and Veracruz.

Mission to Mexico

On October 24, 1956, Frank País journeyed to Mexico to discuss strategy with Fidel. País had been very successful in organizing M-26 cells in various cities in the Oriente province. With the help of Moncada veterans Haydée Santamaría and Lester Rodríguez, his organization had become the M-26's best agency in Cuba. It also provided Fidel with his best source of information. Much of País's success stemmed from his ability to attract young people into the movement, Vilma Espín for one.

Vilma came from a middle-class family, the daughter of a Santiago physician. She graduated from the Massachusetts Institute of Technology in the United States as an engineer. A sworn communist, she worked

Vilma Espín at her wedding to Raúl Castro. Vilma was the only woman to rise to a high position of power in Castro's government.

with a passion to promote an air of rebellion in Oriente. Her politics added weight to a growing body of Marxist thought evolving within the movement. Raúl Castro and Vilma would meet in the Sierra and marry in Santiago shortly after victory. A woman driven to power, she would one day sit as a member of the Cuban Council of State. Ultimately, she would become the only woman member of the Communist Party's Political Bureau—the Party's ruling body—which made her one of the most powerful women in Cuba. Despite her hard work for, and apparent loyalty to, the movement, Frank País never liked or trusted her.

Frank País failed in his mission to Mexico. He had hoped to talk Fidel into putting off the M-26 landing. In an earlier letter to Fidel, Frank had written that his armed groups in Cuba were "unprotected, unprepared, and uncoordinated."[57] Accordingly, Frank believed that they should delay the landing until sometime after the first of the year. His words echoed those of José Antonio Echeverría, leader of the allied Revolutionary Directorate (DR) in Havana. For two reasons of his own, Fidel said no to País.

First, he had announced to the world on several occasions that he would return to Cuba in 1956. (General Bayo had earlier criticized Fidel strongly for so advising the enemy of his plans. Fidel replied, "It is a peculiarity all my own, although I know that militarily it might be harmful. It is psychological warfare."[59] To break his promise would cause him to lose credibility. And second, considering the recent arrests, it was becoming just too dangerous to remain in Mexico much longer.

The *Granma*

A month earlier, Fidel had traveled to McAllen, Texas, to meet with Carlos Prío Socarrás, the former Cuban president. Prío still held fond hopes of returning to Cuba and regaining his office. A man of great wealth, Prío stood for everything Fidel hated. But he shared Fidel's hatred of Batista, and, more important, he had what Fidel needed most: money.

Although ex-president Carlos Prío Socarrás held opposite political ideas from Fidel, Fidel needed his financial support. The two were also united in their hatred of Batista.

Fidel (center) with fellow revolutionaries on board the rickety Granma *in 1959.*

The two men talked for an hour. When they finished, Fidel left with $50,000 of Prío's money, and a promise of $50,000 more. Prío's only condition was that Fidel must agree to join him in a united front against Batista. Fidel had no problem with such an agreement then, nor did he have any problem ignoring it later.

Back in Mexico City, Fidel received a visit from Melba Hernández, who had been working with the M-26 and the DR in Havana. She also made the trip up from Cuba to warn him that few preparations had been made for the landing. Fidel answered her as he had answered País. And he sent her back with the same message for Echeverría: He would return to Cuba before year's end.

Having so committed himself, his next order of business took on an even greater urgency. He needed a boat, and he needed it right away. Fidel picked the small port of Tuxpán on the Gulf of Mexico from which to depart. As luck would have it, he found the *Granma* there, an old and worn wooden boat, only thirty-eight feet long. It was completely unsuited to his needs.

But the moment he saw it, Fidel said, "In this boat, I am going to Cuba."[60] He bought it with no argument from a smiling American owner for $20,000 of Prío's money.

On November 24, 1956, the rebel "invasion force" gathered to embark. Faustino Pérez recalled the scene for Carlos Franqui:

We assembled at night at Tuxpán, on the Gulf of Mexico, a city divided by the river whose name it bears. It was a dark, rainy night. . . . One after the other, the groups came to the prearranged meeting place, using the darkest streets. We were totally convinced of the importance of our mission, and nobody asked questions, or even spoke. . . . When the arms, ammunition, and other military supplies had been loaded, an orderly rush to get on board began. We were afraid that the last ones would have to stay behind. . . . It was 1:00 A.M., November 25, 1956, and time to leave. As quietly as possible, with only one engine going at low speed and all her lights out, the *Granma* began to pull away. . . . We were on course for Cuba, but the hardest part still lay ahead of us.[61]

Chapter

5 The Sierra Maestra: The Fight

After a storm-lashed voyage, Fidel and his eighty-one warriors "landed" at Playa Colorada on Cuba's southeastern coast. They had arrived on December 2, 1956, two days late and about a mile from their intended destination of Niquero. In a swampy location just below the aptly named Purgatory Point, the *Granma* ran afoul of mud and muck. At 4:20 A.M., the shabby little vessel wallowed to a halt some one hundred yards from land.

The "invaders" were forced to wade the rest of the way to shore through hip-deep mud, carrying only their personal weapons. All of their heavy equipment and stores were left behind. Because they had landed in a swamp, it took them two hours to reach firm ground. By then, everyone was exhausted. They had landed late, in the wrong place, and, as yet, nothing had gone right. Not a proud beginning. As Juan Manuel Márquez said later, "It wasn't a landing, it was a shipwreck."[62] And Faustino Pérez recalled that "Fidel looked angry."[63]

Crescencio Pérez and a hundred men had been waiting for Fidel's landing force

near Niquero with several trucks. Fidel's plan called for a dawn attack on Niquero on November 30. They would first secure Niquero, then launch an attack by truck against Manzanillo, before moving from there into the Sierra Maestra. At the same time, Frank País's rebels were scheduled to stage their uprising in nearby Santiago. But it didn't happen that way.

The loyal Frank País initiated his Santiago uprising on November 30 as scheduled. Three hundred or so of his rebels, clad in olive green uniforms and wearing M-26-7 red-and-black armbands, attacked the police station, the Customs House, and the harbor headquarters. The fighting raged for two days. At one point, País and his *Fidelistas* actually controlled the city, but reinforced Batista forces eventually prevailed. When the bloody two-day uprising ended, scores of rebels and soldiers lay dead in the cobbled streets of the old city. Pepito Tey, País's second-in-command, was among the unlucky ones who were killed. Frank País himself escaped to fight another day.

Batista forces learned of Fidel's arrival in Cuba less than two hours after the landing. Although Fidel had lost the all-important element of surprise, he nonetheless felt a strong sense of satisfaction. He had kept his promise to the Cuban people and the world: He had returned to Cuba before the end of 1956.

Like José Martí six decades before, Fidel stood on Oriente's shore, poised and ready to liberate his beloved land. The fight was just beginning. It would last for twenty-five months.

The United Press attempted to alter history on December 4, 1956. A news release written by reporter Francis McCarthy reported the deaths of Fidel Castro and forty M-26 members, including Raúl Castro and Juan Manuel Márquez. Much the same as had once been the case with Mark Twain, reports of their deaths were "greatly exaggerated." Fidel took so unkindly to the report that months later he forced McCarthy to leave Cuba.

But Fidel's invaders soon fell under attack from government planes. Scattered

Fidel and his rebels in the Sierra Maestra. Fidel's first invasion attempt was fraught with error and difficulty.

Fidel in the Sierra Maestra

In Castro's Cuba, Cuba's Fidel, *Lee Lockwood wrote of a conversation with Guillermo García, who was amazed at Fidel's ability to adapt to the Sierra Maestra.*

"Fidel had never been in these mountains before. But in six months he knew the whole Sierra better than any *guajiro* [peasant] who was born here. He never forgot a place that he went to. He remembered everything—the soil, the trees, who lived in each house. In those days, I was a cattle buyer. I used to go all over the mountains. But in six months Fidel knew the Sierra better than I did, and I was born and raised here."

Fidel reads while in the Sierra Maestra in 1957. Castro's confidence in his own destiny seemed unshakable.

and confused, they set out on foot for the safety of the Sierra Maestra. "To avoid the planes," Faustino Pérez wrote, "Fidel ordered rest during the day and marches at night."[64] Three days after their landing, they had managed to trek only a scant twenty-two miles inland.

Arriving at a foothill area called Alegría del Pío on the morning of December 5, the rebels settled in to rest. Shortly after 4:00 P.M., a hail of bullets sprayed their area, followed by a rush of Batista soldiers. Caught by surprise, the rebels again scattered. Fidel kept firing his rifle, while di-

recting his men and calling for a retreat into nearby cane fields. Running hard for their lives, they split into twenty-six separate groups.

Che Guevara took a bullet in the lower shoulder and thought he was going to die.

Immediately, I began to think about the best way of dying in that minute when all seemed lost. I remembered an old story by Jack London in which the [main character], leaning against a tree trunk, prepares to end his life with dignity, knowing he was con-

In Castro's failed invasion attempt, many of his revolutionaries would scatter in the melee that followed, some killed by soldiers, others returning to their homes. Twenty-two (pictured, Fidel marked by arrow) would be arrested and imprisoned.

demned to death in the frozen plains of Alaska. This is the only image I remember.[65]

Luckily for him, the wound wasn't serious and he escaped the trap.

Sixty-six other rebels weren't so fortunate. At least three were killed in the shoot-out. Many died a fiery death when the soldiers set fire to the cane fields where they tried to hide. Juan Manuel Márquez and Níco López, two leaders, were caught and executed. Within two days, twenty-one more were caught and killed. Twenty-two others were caught and sent to prison, and the remainder otherwise disappeared. Some escaped to their homes; others, probably trapped in the cane fields, were never heard from again.

The Twelve

Sixteen men (women of the movement did not take part in the landing) remained to face government forces numbering over forty thousand, not counting the Rural Guard and the National Police. (Fidel recalls only twelve survivors—*Los Doce*—probably more from a flair for drama than an accurate memory: Carlos Manuel de Céspedes, who led the revolt in 1868, continued the fight with twelve men after his first defeat. And, too, the disciples of Jesus numbered twelve.) Included among the survivors were Raúl Castro, Che Guevara, Camilo Cienfuegos, Juan Almeida, Faustino Pérez, and Ramiro Valdés.

Alegría de Pío marked Fidel's first defeat in his renewed fight for freedom. His rebel army all but destroyed, it seemed likely that his revolution was over. But Fidel didn't see things as others saw them. With the help of mountain man Guillermo García—the rebels' first volunteer—he managed to pull his small band back together in the Sierra Maestra.

In the middle of a banana field, Fidel turned to García and asked, "Are we already in the Sierra Maestra?" The mountain man told him that they were. "Then the Revolution has triumphed!" Fidel shouted happily.[66] With childlike enthusiasm, Fidel gushed confidence. He fully believed that the success of his revolution depended on reaching the mountain safely. From the mountains they would fight on to a guerrilla victory.

Years later, García recalled: "You know, Fidel spoke with so much emotion—you had to believe him. Even . . . though it seemed crazy, I believed him."[67]

First Victory

On January 17, 1957, slightly over a month after their setback at Alegría del Pío, the rebels repaid the army in kind with a surprise attack on the garrison at La Plata. Che Guevara described the attack this way:

> It was 2:40 A.M. The soldiers [taken by surprise] were practically defenseless and were being mowed down by our bullets. Camilo Cienfuegos was the first to go in. We took 8 rifles, 1 Thompson machine gun, and 1000 rounds; we had used about 500. Two soldiers were killed and five wounded (three died later); we took three prisoners but let them go. Not a scratch on our side. This was our first victory.[68]

News about Fidel's "death" reached him in February. He immediately sent Faustino Pérez to Havana with orders to "bring back a foreign journalist."[69] Fidel wanted to assure Batista and the world that he was alive and well—and rebelling in Cuba. And he probably remembered the words of Gen. Máximo Gómez, who once said, "Without a press we shall get nowhere."[70]

Faustino called on Celia Sánchez Manduley for assistance. Celia, who would later become the most important person in Fidel's life, had organized M-26-7 activi-

ties in Manzanillo. She arranged through her network for Faustino's safe passage to Havana.

Herbert L. Matthews, the esteemed foreign correspondent for the *New York Times*, jumped at the chance to interview the supposedly dead guerrilla leader. On February 16, 1957, Matthews and his wife Nancie arrived in a jungle clearing, twenty-five miles from the city of Manzanillo. Moments later, Fidel, with his usual flair, appeared dramatically from out of the morning mist.

Deeply impressed by his meeting with Fidel, Matthews wrote:

> The personality of the man is overpowering. It was easy to see that his men adored him and also to see why he has caught the imagination of the youth of Cuba all over the island. Here was an

Celia Sánchez Manduley arranged for a reporter to meet with Castro in the jungle.

educated, dedicated fanatic, a man of ideals, of courage and of remarkable qualities of leadership.[71]

Stories persist even now that Fidel tricked Matthews into believing—and reporting—that the rebel army was much stronger than it really was. Fidel supposedly paraded the same few men in and out of the clearing, again and again, to give the look of greater numbers. But Matthews defended his reporting.

"If these things did take place they made no impression of any kind on me," he wrote later.[72]

Without regard to whether he was deceived about the strength of the rebel army, Matthews correctly concluded: "From the look of things, General Batista cannot possibly hope to suppress the Castro revolt. His only hope is that an Army column will come upon the young rebel leader and his staff and wipe them out. This is hardly likely to happen."[73]

The young rebel leader couldn't have asked for more. When Matthews's article appeared in the *New York Times* on the following Sunday, it focused the eyes of the world squarely on Fidel Castro. And that's precisely where he wanted them.

Until its publication, Fidel had been little more than a name to the people of Cuba. Matthews established the romantic image of Fidel as the bearded, rifle-bearing guerrilla leader, clad in olive-drab fatigues and fighting the good fight. This new image brought far-reaching recognition, new volunteers, and added support to Fidel and his movement. It also provided Cubans a figure to identify with and rally around. In all, Matthews wrote three articles about Fidel in the Sierra Maestra. The articles didn't guarantee Fidel's success,

but few things aided his cause more than the myth established by Matthews.

Over the next two years, the rebels implemented the revolution in various ways. Dictated by terrain and situation, their activities assumed two basic forms: the *llano*, or lowlands (or urban revolution), and the *sierra* (or mountain revolution). Varying conditions demanded different operating methods and required that orders of importance be established. This opened the door for more than one revolutionary leader.

One Leader

Fidel never for an instant considered sharing the leadership of *his* revolution. He

Fidel managed to fool the Cuban government into believing his rebel forces were much larger and stronger than they really were.

had said more than once that "a revolution must have only one leader if it is to remain whole and not be defeated. One bad leader is better than twenty good ones."[74]

Throughout the course of the Cuban Revolution, Fidel faced continual challenges to his insistence on sole leadership. His chief opposition came from José Antonio Echeverría, leader of the Revolutionary Directorate (DR) based in Havana. (There were other, lesser challenges to Fidel's leadership too numerous to mention.) The DR formed a major part of the *llano* (or urban) branch of revolutionaries, separate and distinct from the M-26-7 *sierra* branch. (The Revolutionary Directorate should not be confused with the National Directorate, a loose network of revolutionary leaders that attempted to unify rebel activities throughout the island.) Although equally dedicated to bringing down the Batista regime, the DR views of how the revolution should be conducted differed greatly from Fidel's. In short, the DR didn't recognize Fidel's claim to a single leadership.

On February 20, 1957, to strengthen his position as the sole leader, he issued an "Appeal to the People of Cuba." The "Appeal" contained brief accounts of rebel victories at La Plata and Palma Mocha, as well as other rebel actions. Most important, it set forth guidelines for conducting the revolution. His guidelines included the burning of cane fields, sabotage, execution of certain enemies, civil resistance, raising money to support the movement, and strikes. By issuing this appeal, Fidel knew that challengers to his leadership must either follow his guidelines (and thus accept him as sole leader) or confront him openly. José Echeverría stepped forth to confront him.

Attack on the Presidential Palace

On the night of March 12, 1957, DR leader Echeverría issued a manifesto that said in part:

> We ask our comrades, the students of all Cuba, to organize, since they constitute the vanguard [the leaders] of our struggle, and we ask the armed forces to remember that their mission is to defend their homeland, not to oppress their brothers; and that their task is that of the *mambí* army [*mambís*, blacks descended from slaves, constituted a major part of the army] which fought [in 1895] for THE LIBERTY OF CUBA, as they affirm at the end of all their writings.
>
> Viva Cuba Libre! [Long live free Cuba!][75]

It was a broad appeal for a student uprising, coupled with a plea to Batista's army not to interfere. It was also Echeverría's claim to revolutionary leadership.

On the following day, members of the DR attacked the Presidential Palace in Havana in an attempt to assassinate Batista. Two heavily armed groups mounted the attack. The first group of fifty men was led by Carlos Gutiérrez Menoya, a Spaniard who had fought against Franco in the 1930s and the Nazis during World War II. Heading the second group was former Auténtico congressman Mora Morales. His group numbered about one hundred students and was meant to back up and support Gutiérrez's people. Echeverría himself led a small party to seize control of the Radio Reloj radio station. He hoped to broadcast news of Batista's death

On March 12, 1957, members of the Revolutionary Directorate (DR), a rival rebel group, attacked the Presidential Palace in hopes of assassinating Batista.

and an appeal for Cubans to take up arms and join the revolution. A fourth group was sent to halt the flow of incoming and outgoing traffic at the Havana airport.

The DR expected to form a revolutionary government in the aftermath of the attack. Significantly, they neither informed the M-26-7 of their plans nor invited the movement's participation.

The attack on the palace commenced at 3:24 P.M., a time when Batista was usually in his second-floor office. But on this day, Batista's son lay sick in the living quarters of the palace on the third floor. Batista had taken the elevator—the only access to the third floor—to check on his son. The elevator was still on the third floor when the attackers struck with automatic weapons and grenades. They searched through the palace in desperation but couldn't find a way to the third floor. When guards on the roof sprayed the inside patio and the surrounding streets with machine-gun fire, the attackers started to back off. A few escaped but most were killed in the palace.

Meanwhile, Echeverría succeeded in taking over the radio station not far from the palace. Excitedly, he shouted a message to soldiers, sailors, police officers,

and Cubans at large to join the battle for freedom. Unfortunately for Echeverría and his cause, he had been speaking into a dead microphone. An automatic cut-off device was installed in the microphone to prevent damage to broadcasting equipment when someone spoke too loudly. No one had heard him. Nor did he know that the attack on the palace had failed. Echeverría's luck ran out entirely when he left the radio station. In his haste to join the others in revolt, his car smashed into a police patrol car. He jumped out and started firing his machine gun at the police. They returned his fire. José Antonio Echeverría, Fidel's strongest rival, died instantly.

Batista brought troops from Camp Columbia by the thousands into the streets of Havana. Tanks ringed the palace grounds. And the Cuban people, looking after their own best interests, rose in support of the powerful Batista forces. The revolt ended quickly.

The failed attack delivered a stunning blow to the urban revolutionaries. Thirty-five DR members were killed, and scores of others were caught, tortured, and murdered by Batista forces intent on revenge. It is not likely, however, that Fidel Castro in his mountain stronghold mourned the loss of Echeverría.

The Strange Death of Frank País

In the spring of 1957, Frank País began to challenge Fidel's role as sole leader. País proposed opening a second front in the Sierra Cristal, northeast of Santiago, with himself in charge. He also proposed a change in the structure of the movement's National Directorate, then overly crowded with leaders scattered around the island. The proposal would elevate País to an equal leadership level with Fidel. Fidel, recognizing the latest threat to his leadership, declined to act on País's suggestions. A rift quickly developed between the two men.

On July 30, 1957, Frank País was gunned down in Santiago's Callejó del Muro by police chief Col. José Salas Cañizares and one of his men known as "Mano Negra"—Black Hand. Only moments before, País, while in hiding, had received a phone call from Vilma Espín. Movement members knew that the police monitored all phone calls and so used the phone only for emergencies.

Vilma called Frank only to ask, "Why have you not called me? What has happened?"[76] Such a call hardly seemed necessary.

In any event, Frank País's death erased still another threat to Fidel's leadership. And the ambitious Vilma replaced País as head of the movement in Santiago. It has never been proven that Vilma phoned Frank that day so that police might locate País by means of a phone tap. But it is safe to say that his death gave a boost to her rise in the movement. And though nothing has ever connected Fidel with País's death, it would seem unlikely that Fidel mourned the passing of another rival for very long.

Coming of Age

Earlier, a battle at El Uvero, west of Santiago on the southern coast of Oriente province, marked the *sierra* group's first important victory. On May 28, 1957, the rebels attacked an army garrison, seized many weapons, and disappeared back into the hills. Of the action, Che Guevara wrote:

> Our guerrilla force came of age. From the time of that combat, our morale rose enormously, our determination and our hopes of triumph also grew with that victory, and although the suc-

Vilma Espín (right) pictured with Celia Sánchez. Vilma has been implicated in the death of Castro's rival Frank País.

ceeding months were a hard trial, we were already in possession of the secret victory over the enemy.[77]

In September, a rebel attempt to take over the naval base at Cienfuegos failed. But on September 10, Fidel's *sierra* fighters deliberately ambushed Batista forces for the first time at Pino del Agua, a tiny town in the deep woods. The guerrilla victory there established a turning point in the revolution.

Rebel Reign of Terror

November marked the beginning of a rebel reign of terror, as the *Fidelistas* set torch to Cuba's cane fields. This tactic, of course, had been called for earlier in Fidel's "Appeal to the People of Cuba." They started the torching at Lina Castro's plantation. Fidel could hardly spare his family lands from the torch while the rest

of Oriente burned. Scores of people died in the flames that burned from one end of the island to the other. Fidel and his mother would never again share a close relationship.

In Miami, Cuban politicians from seven groups that opposed Fidel gathered to form what later was called the "Miami Pact." Revolutionaries other than members of the 26th of July Movement persisted in their attempts to gain a share in the revolution's leadership. The pact proposed, among other things, that a Cuban Liberation group be formed to create a regular army after the fall of Batista. A standing army under their control would clearly provide them with the force of arms necessary to control Fidel.

Fidel, who was not represented at their meeting, rejected their agreement out of hand. He declared with vigor that "the 26th of July Movement claims for itself the function of maintaining public order and reorganizing the armed forces of the Republic." He went on to say that "while the

Attack on the Presidential Palace

Faure Chomón, a Revolutionary Directorate leader, described the plan to attack the Presidential Palace in Havana on March 13, 1957, in Carlos Franqui's book Diary of the Cuban Revolution.

"The operations to launch the action would be threefold: first, the assault on the Presidential Palace [to assassinate Batista] by a squad of fifty men; the second, an operation to back up this commando squad, in which more than a hundred men would take part; and third, the taking of the Radio Reloj radio station in order to broadcast news of Batista's death and address the people, while the commando squad that had taken the station would go on to the university, where our general headquarters would be installed."

Fearing for her life, Celia (behind Fidel) joined him in the Sierra at the end of 1957. They became close friends and associates until her death in 1980.

leaders of the other organizations who [signed] the pact are abroad fighting an imaginary revolution, the leaders of the 26th of July Movement are in Cuba, making a real revolution."[78] Without the support of the rebel army, the Miami Pact died for lack of further attention.

Fearing discovery and capture by the police in Manzanillo, Celia Sánchez joined Fidel in the Sierra at the end of 1957. She would remain at his side during the rest of the fighting and for a long time after. It is known that Sánchez became his very dearest friend and most trusted advisor until she died of cancer on January 11, 1980. Fidel was shattered by her death.

At the beginning of 1958, more guerrillas—the remains of Echeverría's Revolutionary Directorate—began operations against Batista in the Escambray Mountains of central Cuba. Lacking the strong leadership of a Fidel Castro, however, they eventually split into two groups. In the end, they were more than willing to restore complete leadership of the revolution to Fidel.

Then it became Raúl Castro's turn to lead. Fidel put his brother in charge of opening a second front in Oriente. It was the same second front in the Sierra Cristal that Frank País had pushed to open months before. In 1958, between March 1 and December 31, Raúl's guerrillas engaged Batista's army on some 247 occasions. They racked up a kill ratio of twelve soldiers to one rebel. This experience as a leader laid a foundation for Raúl's later role as General of the Army.

Nor did Raúl confine himself solely to military activities. He loved to experiment with new revolutionary methods, such as hijacking and international kidnapping. On one occasion, for example, his guerrillas seized a busload of American sailors and Marines near Guantánamo City. They then demanded that the United States stop supplying arms to Batista. Eventually, their demands were met and they released all their prisoners without harm, but not before they had again drawn the world's attention to their cause. Latter-day terrorists and political thugs would

Raúl Castro (center) surrounded by aides and commanders. Raúl was put in charge of organizing the second rebel front, out of Oriente. Not content to merely stage guerrilla attacks, Raúl also ordered kidnappings and hijackings.

use Raúl's innovative methods to great advantage.

Raúl further demonstrated his versatility by forming a peasant intelligence unit, which later evolved into Fidel's own G-2 intelligence agency. And with the help of José Ramírez Cruz—the first communist to join the *sierra* rebels—Raúl started organizing the peasants politically. Together, Raúl and José formed a school of political thought to shape rural minds for the future. Their school introduced the first communist text used in Cuba.

Although Raúl's politics ran along Communist Party lines, he didn't try to force his political views on Fidel. He preferred to withhold his thoughts until the right moment came along. At that point, two options—either a democratic or a communist form of government—remained opened to Fidel. The "right" moment would come later. Fidel, motivated by his deep-rooted need to acquire absolute power, would come to recognize that communism would serve that need

better. And it would assure his lifelong position as head of the new Cuban state.

The Strike That Failed

On April 9, 1958, the *llano* broadcast a call to strike over several Havana radio stations: "Attention Cubans! Attention Cubans! This is the 26th of July calling a general revolutionary strike. Today is the day of liberation."[79] And from the *sierra*, the radio cried: "Strike! Strike! Strike! Everyone strike! Everyone into the streets!"[80]

The rebels hoped to paralyze the Batista-run state. But the dictator responded swiftly and severely, issuing an order to kill anyone connected with the strike. As a result, at least 140 youths died, slain by police under the command of Chief Pilar García. The strike failed badly, signaling the end of the *llano* leadership.

On April 10, Fidel issued a message declaring, "All Cuba burns and erupts in an explosion of anger against the assassins, the bandits and gangsters, the informers, the strikebreakers, the thugs and the military still loyal to Batista."[81] This was more sound and fury than truth because by then any hope of a strike had passed. But once and for all, Fidel took full control of the revolution.

A Communist Influence

In the late spring, Carlos Rafael Rodríguez—a leading Cuban communist thinker—joined Fidel in the mountains. Carlos Rafael kept close company with Fidel until the revolution triumphed. All during this time, he found Fidel to be more than willing to listen to his communist teachings. In later years, Carlos Rafael used his influence to keep Fidel's thinking in line with communist ideology.

Carlos Rafael Rodríguez joined the Fidelistas *and introduced them to the thoughts of communist le[...] Mao Tse-tung.*

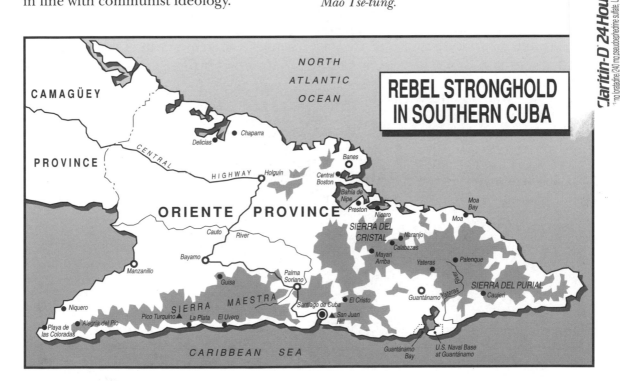

REBEL STRONGHOLD
IN SOUTHERN CUBA

Carlos Rafael also influenced the tactics being used by the *Fidelistas* in the mountains: With him he brought the writings of Mao Tse-tung on guerrilla warfare. Che proceeded from that point to use Mao's tactics against Batista's forces with great success. Che later wrote his own book on the subject.

By June of 1958, the *barbudos*—the bearded guerrillas—occupied or controlled most of the mountain areas of Oriente province. (Their beards had become something of a legend. During their training under Bayo, he had told them that "no guerrilla shaves, nor cleans his teeth."[82] They held true to his code.) Fidel had by then established a headquarters in a large, rambling wooden house in La Plata, the site of the rebels' first victory. Not the Havana Hilton, but conditions were improving.

In the summer of 1958, Batista launched what was to become his last-gasp offensive. A Batista force led by Gen. Eulogio Cantillo surrounded most of Fidel's guerrillas in late July and threatened to turn back the revolutionary tide. Fidel, realizing that most of his men were in danger of being wiped out, sent a messenger to Cantillo's camp. Fidel called for a ceasefire with talks to follow. To the amazement and ire of most of Cantillo's officers, Cantillo agreed to the talks.

The general sent Lt. Col. Fernando Neugart to talk terms with Fidel. But Fidel did all the talking. For three days, he talked, and talked, and talked, in what Neugart later called an "endless speech" against Batista's government.[83] And while Fidel talked, most of his men slipped through the ring of Cantillo's forces and lived to fight some more. Batista's offensive petered out by the end of summer.

Rebel Blitzkrieg

The rebels then stepped up their attacks on the peripheries of the Sierra. In September, Che Guevara and Camilo Cienfuegos led their men westward in an offensive

By mid-November 1958 Fidel's rebels were able to seize all the rail and bus transportation in Oriente and make lightning-quick attacks throughout Cuba, including at the national army post in Santa Clara (left).

Che's Three Points for Guerrilla Warfare

After his experiences in the Sierra Maestra, Che Guevara summed up briefly what he learned about guerrilla fighting in his book Pasajes de la Guerra Revolucionaria.

"I limited myself to recommending emphatically three points: constant mobility, constant distrust, constant vigilance. Mobility means never to stay in the same place; not to spend two nights at the same spot; never to stop marching from one place to another. Distrust—from the very beginning distrust your own shadow, your peasant friends, your informers, your guides, your contacts; distrust everything until you have established a free zone. Vigilance—sentry posts at all times, constant patrols, encampments only in a secure place and, above all these things, never sleep under a roof, never sleep in a house that can be surrounded."

that shortly became known as the "Westward March of Che and Camilo." Batista's forces started to fade in front of the rebel advance. Some refused to continue the fight. Others defected.

The rebel army accelerated its offensive and raced across Cuba with a speed not unlike Hitler's blitzkrieg during World War II. By mid-November 1958, they commanded all of the rail and bus transportation in Oriente. In December, they swept through towns, army posts, and cities in their lightning advance: La Maya, Alto Songo, San Luis, Ermita, Miranda, Alto Cedro, Marcané, Borgitas, Algodonal, Santa Clara. By year's end, the columns of Che and Camilo paused at the outskirts of Havana. At the same time, Fidel and his men closed in on Santiago, where it had all begun.

In twenty-five months, Fidel Castro had come a long way toward fulfilling his destiny and the promise of "The Apostle," José Martí: He had defeated Batista's military might; seized control of the *llano*, the city arm of the 26th of July Movement; stripped the old political parties of their power; overcome U.S. support of Batista and rejected U.S. influence in Cuban affairs; and built a following that would implement his vision of a "new Cuba." These were astonishing accomplishments. Yet much remained to be done.

As Fidel said in his first speech to the Cuban people on entering Santiago, "The Revolution begins now."[84]

6 Rebels in Havana: The Revolution

With the rebel columns of Che Guevara and Camilo Cienfuegos sweeping toward Havana, President Fulgencio Batista celebrated New Year's Eve of 1959 by hosting a party at the Presidential Palace. At 2:00 A.M., he left the party to meet in private with his military commanders. At 3:00 A.M., Batista resigned as president and flew out of Havana, bound for the Dominican Republic, with his wife and three of his children. On the night of January 1, the *barbudos* of Guevara and Cienfuegos entered Havana in triumph.

Earlier that same day, 163,000 residents of Santiago turned out at 1:00 A.M. to wildly greet Fidel and his bearded warriors. The fighting was over. The rebel army, numbering somewhere between two and three thousand volunteers, had defeated Batista's regular army of approximately forty-six thousand soldiers.

"On January 2, at the University of Santiago, [Manuel] Urrutia was proclaimed president," wrote Carlos Franqui, "and that night Fidel made a speech in which he said: 'Now the Revolution is a reality.'"[85] Fidel's impossible dream had come true.

Fidel then moved across the length of the island, traveling by jeep and helicopter. He paused here and there along the way to savor his victory. He finally en-

Castro's troops parade through Havana after the defeat of Batista.

Fidelito atop the victory tank in Havana on January 8, 1959.

tered Havana on January 8, 1959, on the back of a tank. His son Fidelito rode beside him on the tank. Camilo Cienfuegos and Huber Matos, another rebel leader, followed close behind. The "liberators" paraded down the wide streets of Havana through cheering crowds of more than a million people.

Later, Fidel addressed *las masas*—the crowd—from the terrace of the Presidential Palace: "We had a quieter life in the hills than we are going to have from now on. Now, we are going to purify the country."[86] Few among the happy throng attached any forbidding meaning to the words of this man who so commanded their attention and awe.

Ruby Hart Phillips, the *New York Times* bureau chief in Cuba, described how Fidel charmed the people: "As I watched Castro I realized the magic of his personality. He seemed to weave a hypnotic net over his listeners, making them believe in his own concept of the functions of Government and the destiny of Cuba."[87]

Noting the crowd reactions to Fidel, John Topping, the political officer at the American embassy, said, "This guy knows how to press the button."[88]

Fidel used his talent well. He swiftly won the support of the people, in no small part because of his many speeches and public appearances. They willingly accepted his promises of better days ahead. Psychiatrist Jerrold Post observed that Fidel's speeches seemed to say, "Follow me, and I will take care of you."[89]

Fidel also knew how to take care of his enemies. Another side to Fidel's character surfaced early in his rise to power. He acted right away to eliminate potential rivals for control of the country. When gentle persuasion or manipulation failed to remove pretenders to his leadership, he didn't hesitate to use violence.

¡Paredón!

Fidel purged and executed untold numbers of *Batistianos*, whom he considered to be "war criminals"; political opponents and would-be threats to his power base received similar treatment. Mock trials became commonplace, as did cries of "*¡Paredón!—To the Wall!*" [to face the firing squad]. Newspapers in the United States and Mexico criticized the trials and executions. Wayne Morse, a U.S. senator from Oregon, urged an end to the "Cuban bloodbath" and suggested U.S. intervention.

An angry Fidel replied that justice would proceed "until all criminals of the Batista regime are tried" and that "if the Americans don't like what's happening in Cuba, they can land the Marines and then there will be 200,000 *gringos* dead."[90]

Any attempt to judge Fidel's use of violence should be approached with the understanding that revolution itself is the ultimate violence of a people. Revolutions are most often born in violence and equally often prevail by violence. And the pain of insecurity that dwells within most revolutionary rulers seems to compel them to enact the sure and swift elimination of their enemies. If this be the nature of the revolutionary, Fidel fits the role.

CIA director Allen Dulles, appearing before the U.S. Senate Foreign Relations Committee, recommended restraint:

> When you have a revolution, you kill your enemies. There were many instances of cruelty and oppression by the Cuban army, and they have the goods on some of those people. Now there probably will be a lot of justice. It will probably go much too far, but they have to go through this.[91]

The United States kept hands off, and Cuban "justice" prevailed. Fidel later admitted executing at least 550 Batista "criminals." His justice carried over to once-loyal followers from the Sierra. Anyone who spoke or acted against him or his policies was imprisoned, executed, or banished. It should be said that those executed were truly believed to have committed large-scale crimes or brutalities. Some of these

As in many other revolutions, shortly after his victory Fidel announced that he planned to assassinate his political opponents, dubbing them "war criminals."

crimes might appear to be undeserving of harsh punishment. Right or wrong, however, the revolutionary's survival depends on strict enforcement of accepted rules. Under revolutionary law established and documented in the Sierra in 1958, such acts—however trivial they might appear—were declared punishable by death.

Purification Process

Although Urrutia served as president, Fidel, as commander in chief of the armed services, made all the important decisions. On February 16, 1959, Fidel took the oath of office and became prime minister. By then, the Cuban people had begun referring to him as their "maximum leader," and he fully intended to lead them.

He established the top three penthouse floors of the Havana Hilton as a headquarters and began his "purification" process. His first acts were to clamp down hard on prostitution, gambling, and drug trafficking. And he set out immediately to change the old social order in Cuba. But nothing came easy. Those who knew him well noticed that the once jovial Fidel seldom smiled anymore.

Despite the long years under Batista's rule, Cuba's national income stood at $2,311,200,000 in 1957. Only the much larger countries of Mexico, Argentina, and Venezuela boasted greater wealth. But Cuba owed much of its income to gambling, drugs, and prostitution—the same vices that Fidel was doing his best to rid the country of. Cuba's new rulers would have to find some way to replace them as a source of income. And quickly.

Mounting Problems

But Fidel and his *barbudos* knew little about running a government. What they learned, they learned largely by trial and error. "The more problems we solve," he told author Conte Agüero, "the more problems appear."[92] A shortage of oil in Cuba and sorry relations with the United States represented two cases in point. In January, just ten days after taking power in Havana, Fidel had flown to Venezuela to discuss both problems with Rómulo Betancourt, president of the oil-rich nation.

At this point, Fidel held only the vaguest idea of how to deal with the economic problems facing him at home. But he seemed to not allow himself to fret over internal problems, as if somehow they would solve themselves. He viewed himself as the Simón Bolívar of the twentieth century and was apparently obsessed with leading Latin America away from Yankee exploitation. His first step was to seek both financial and political support.

Betancourt had helped Fidel in the Sierra Maestra and also (according to Fidel) in his Dominican expedition, but not this time. Fidel had long held the idea of exporting the "blessings" of his revolution to other Third World countries. He wanted to organize all South American countries in a "continental revolt" against U.S. influence. Betancourt, unmoved by the Cuban leader's ideas, turned a deaf

Although Manuel Urrutia (seated) was ostensibly president of Cuba, Castro (speaking) was really the man in power.

ear to Fidel's request for aid and support. Fidel returned to Havana with little to show for his trip.

Problems persisted for the new regime. The promise of elections within a year was delayed. In April 1959, Ernesto Che Guevara said, "Elections will be held at the appropriate time; now the people want revolution first and elections later."[93] By fall, elections would be put off for two more years, and then delayed again to some unnamed date in the future.

By late spring, Fidel started to reach out—first to South America, then to Eastern bloc countries. He disliked and distrusted his giant neighbor to the north—echoing the feelings of his model José Martí earlier. Most of Cuba's economic woes, he felt, stemmed from the capitalistic, colonialistic, imperialistic *norteamericanos* (North Americans). Fidel and his young followers had seen and studied how Cuba had become a nation of "haves and have-nots" under a corrupt democratic system. "If this is democracy and capitalism," they said, "we don't want them."[94] Fidel hoped to establish a base of support with sympathetic South American and European countries. This would enable him to sever all ties with the United States. To this end, he sent Che Guevara to South America and Europe to represent him and set his ideas in motion.

Fidel Inside the Monster

At the same time, members of the American Society of Newspaper Editors (ASNE) invited Fidel to attend their annual meeting in Washington, D.C., on April 17, 1959. He accepted the invitation and flew to the United States with a party of about seventy. His trip contributed little toward improving U.S. and Cuban relations. Mostly, it served only to draw world attention to his revolution and *barbudo* image.

Although U.S. aid was clearly available, Fidel shunned it. He felt sure—and rightly so—that U.S. aid would come tied to continued U.S. influence in Cuban affairs. On the flight to Washington, he told Cuban finance minister Rufo López-Fresquet:

> I don't want this trip to be like that of other Latin American leaders who always come to the U.S. to ask for money. I want this to be a goodwill trip. Besides, the Americans will be surprised. And when we go back to Cuba, they will offer us aid without our asking for it. Consequently, we will be in a better bargaining position.[95]

Fidel wanted no strings attached.

Castro tried to solicit financial and political support from Venezuelan president Rómulo Betancourt. Betancourt, however, did not agree with Castro's ideas on fomenting revolution.

Later, when U.S. under-secretary of state Roy Rubottom hinted at possible U.S. aid to Cuba, Fidel stopped him. "No, we are proud to be independent," he said, "and have no intention of asking anyone for anything."[96] The United States took him at his word and didn't offer anything. Many historians still believe that the United States should have offered aid, even if Cuba didn't ask for it.

While in Washington, Fidel attended a luncheon at the Statler-Hilton hosted by acting secretary of state Christian Herter. William Wieland was introduced as "the man in charge of Cuban affairs," to Fidel. Fidel barely managed a smile and said, "I thought that I was in charge of Cuban affairs."[97]

Fidel later appeared before the U.S. Senate Foreign Relations Committee. He assured its members in positive terms that his government in Cuba would continue to take part in the mutual defense of the Western Hemisphere. American and other foreign interests, he added, would remain fully protected in Cuba.

Next, Fidel met for two-and-a-half hours on a quiet Sunday afternoon with Vice President Richard M. Nixon. The vice president later voiced mixed opinions about the Cuban leader. "My first impression of him was that he was simply an idealistic and impractical young man," he told Georgie Anne Geyer. Nixon recalled that he "respected him as a strong personality. He was someone I'd like to have on our side. Castro was worth two hours."[98]

Fidel left Washington somewhat miffed that President Dwight D. Eisenhower wasn't there to honor him officially as Cuba's new prime minister. Eisenhower, when he learned of Fidel's schedule, had opted instead to play golf in Atlanta.

On his return to Cuba, Fidel announced his Agrarian Reform Bill, which sounded at first as if it would greatly benefit

Castro and Vice President Richard Nixon meet during Castro's trip to Washington. Nixon remembered him as idealistic and impractical.

the people. In reality, it only transferred land ownership from private interests (American and other foreign interests included) to the Cuban government. (Continued private ownership might have been more effective and profitable in the long term but at the cost of continuing ties to the United States. Severing such ties was Fidel's main purpose in nationalizing all private interests.) To help effect the enormous changes made necessary by the bill, Fidel established the National Institute of Agrarian Reform (INRA). INRA, in turn, provided Fidel with a means of conducting what has been called his "hidden government."

As INRA's president, Fidel acted at once to tie the reform movement to the rebel army. This connection again strengthened Fidel's position and allowed him to make important economic and political decisions almost at will.

INRA's executive director Antonio Nuñez Jiménez recalled that "Fidel dupli-

Governing from the Shadows

With "figurehead" presidents (Urretia and Dorticós) in place, Castro ruled Cuba by means of a "hidden government." Historian Hugh Thomas outlines the process in his book The Cuban Revolution.

"INRA, the Agrarian Reform Institute, became quickly the main agency of the new government, for its task was not only to [secure] and redistribute land, but to organize road-building, health, education, and housing in the country. INRA was also given a credit department, and it absorbed Sugar, Rice and Coffee Stabilization Institutes. It became, indeed, a kind of shadow government of its own. Under it, the country was divided into twenty-eight zones of different sizes, each commanded by an officer of the rebel army. Castro was president of the INRA."

Castro signs the Agrarian Reform Bill, which seized Cuban land owned by foreign interests and made it the property of the Cuban government. The bill did little to help the average Cuban.

cated in INRA the most important functions of the Revolutionary Government."[99]

One of the first of those functions was what amounted to a second ministry of industry, headed by Che Guevara. Che then stood responsible for Cuba's industrial development, a task wholly unsuited to his abilities, as later confirmed by his failures.

With the help of Raúl Castro, INRA then created its own armed one-hundred-thousand-man militia. INRA funds were used to finance military training, highway construction, peasant housing, and tourist attractions.

In one of what Nuñez Jiménez called "secret speeches," Fidel declared that the institute "is a political instrument and the apparatus for activating the country's masses to carry out a task and to defend this task." Fidel went on to say, "An armed people is the definitive guarantee of the Revolution, precisely because it is armed."[100] With guns behind him, Fidel forged ahead in yet another move to unify his power base.

Eliminating Obstacles

In July 1959, he replaced President Manuel Urrutia, who had become an "obstacle on the road to revolution." At the urging of Che Guevara, Fidel named Osvaldo Dorticós Torrado, a Communist, as the next "figurehead" president. Cuba began to lean more toward communism.

Two more major "obstacles" were eliminated during the first autumn of the revolution in the persons of Camilo Cienfuegos and Huber Matos. Both men were former loyal leaders from the Sierra.

Matos, who was then managing the cattle-rich province of Camagüey, complained to Fidel about Communist Party activities there. He had begun to question Fidel's leadership. He had also protested when Fidel tried forty-three Batista airmen twice for the same offense. When he refused an order from Raúl Castro, Raúl blasted Matos as a traitor before the Council of Ministers in Havana. Matos then offered to resign. In a letter to Fidel, he spoke "off the record."

> It seems right and proper for me to point out that great men become smaller when they start to be unjust. You should remember that men fade away, while history collects their deeds and makes the final reckoning, the final judgment. Now, Fidel, you are destroying your own work. You are burying the revolution. Perhaps there is still time. I plead with you, comrade. Help us save the revolution.[101]

Fidel answered in part, "I am under no obligation to account to you for my actions, and you have no right to judge or prejudge me. If anyone has been disloyal, it has been you."[102]

Matos was then tried for treason. Camilo Cienfuegos spoke out in behalf of Matos but to no avail. Matos was sentenced to twenty years in prison. Fidel appointed Cienfuegos to succeed Matos in Camagüey. On October 28, Cienfuegos flew out of Camagüey on a return flight to Havana. His Cessna 310 disappeared and was never seen or heard from again. On his release from prison, Matos left Cuba for the United States.

The bombshell exploded in Cuba on February 4, 1960.

Communists in Cuba

At Fidel's invitation, Soviet first deputy premier Anastas I. Mikoyan arrived in Havana. During his visit, Mikoyan signed a limited trade agreement between Cuba and the USSR. Soon after his visit, the two countries resumed formal relations, which

The plane of Camilo Cienfuegos, a loyal Castro supporter, mysteriously disappeared without a trace in 1959.

had been severed in 1952. Fidel sent Che Guevara on a mission to the Soviet Union. While there, Che signed several economic agreements with the Soviets. Cuba's shift from West to East gathered speed.

Cuba's relations with the United States started further downhill in March. Within months, Fidel, contrary to his earlier promises, seized control of all American properties in Cuba, mainly sugar mills, oil refineries, and utility companies.

On July 6, 1960, President Eisenhower cut off all sugar imports from Cuba. "This action amounts to economic sanctions against Castro," Eisenhower said. "Now we must look ahead to other moves—economic, diplomatic, strategic."[103]

Three days later, Soviet Premier Nikita Khrushchev announced to the world: "The U.S.S.R. is raising its voice and extending a helpful hand to the people of Cuba. Speaking figuratively, in case of necessity, Soviet artillerymen can support the Cuban people with rocket fire."[104] Fidel later played down the Soviet's reference to rockets, but the world had already begun to wonder.

Khrushchev followed up with a direct message to Fidel: "The Soviet Government wishes to express to you that it does not consider any party as an intermediary between it and you. Comrade Khrushchev considers you to be the authentic leader of the Revolution."[105] Fidel liked that.

Khrushchev's message showed clearly that the Soviets vested all power in Fidel—and denied any power to the Communist Party. This is precisely what Fidel wanted, and what he knew the United States would never concede to him: recognition of his full authority without threat of outside interference into his affairs.

Quickly, then, he began to restructure the country by forming a Central Planning Board to unify economic power (as

in Eastern bloc countries). Next, for reasons evident in its name, he created a Board for Revolutionary Propaganda. Students, workers, and peasants flocked into the swelling ranks of his civilian militia. Finally, he welcomed Soviet military units into Cuba to train and equip the Cuban armed forces.

Dance with a Russian Bear

In September, Fidel returned to the United States to explain his revolution on the floor of the United Nations. While in New York, he met the Soviet premier for the first time. Nikita and Fidel didn't shake hands in the removed way of North Americans. Instead, they hugged each other in the warmer manner of Europeans.

Of their meeting, Khrushchev said, "He bent down and enveloped me with his whole body." Later, he described Fidel as "an heroic man who has raised his people

Castro shakes hands with Soviet first deputy premier Anastas I. Mikoyan in Havana in 1960. Mikoyan's visit began the long relationship between Cuba and the USSR that would also launch the beginning of U.S. worries about Cuba.

from the tyranny of Batista and who has provided a better life for his people. I salute Fidel Castro and wish him well."[106] Cuba's dance with the Russian bear began in earnest.

Responding quickly to the shaping of events in Cuba, the United States recalled its ambassador on October 18, 1960. The next day, President Eisenhower cut off the delivery of certain foods, medicines, and medical supplies to Cuba. This, in effect, established a blockade. The United States would register its ultimate distaste for Fidel's leftist leanings by severing diplomatic ties with Cuba on January 16, 1961.

Fidel now faced a formidable task in his still-developing country, complicated by a number of elements. For example,

Death of a Hero

Mystery has surrounded the death of Camilo Cienfuegos for many years. In his book Fidel Castro, *historian Robert E. Quirk reveals what is likely the real reason for the hero's death.*

Castro critics had long blamed Cienfuego's mysterious death on the Cuban leader.

"Having completed his business in Camagüey late in the afternoon of October 28, Cienfuegos took off in his Cessna 310 for the return flight to Havana. A few minutes later the air force base near Camagüey was advised that an unidentified small plane, presumably from the United States, had been seen firebombing cane fields in the area. A Sea Fury, armed with four 20-mm cannons, was dispatched to intercept it. The Cuban fighter pilot returned some time later and reported that he had shot down the intruder. . . . [Other] explanations cropped up for years: Cienfuegos had been eliminated by the Castro brothers because he was too popular. He had left Cuba and was seen in the United States. His plane had headed east, not west, and crashed in the sea, and the body of the pilot had washed ashore in the Dominican Republic. The fact was that the Cessna had been downed [mistakenly] by the Sea Fury."

Castro found a formidable friend in Nikita Khrushchev, premier of the Soviet Union. The friendship between the nations made U.S. leaders fear for the safety of the United States.

Cuba's economy had previously depended on sugar exports to a lopsided extreme. Her social structure comprised another extreme of haves and have-nots. Historically, she relied on the United States for the now-discontinued goods and services. Each of these elements represented a unique set of problems. Responsibility for solving them rested squarely on the shoulders of rank beginners.

When an existing economic structure is destroyed, a new one must be built to replace it—brick by painful brick—from the ground up. Fidel, of necessity, became the architect for a total restructuring of every section of Cuba's economy. Administration, agriculture, industry, labor, new business, pricing, marketing, financing,

the retraining of workers—all these and more—had to be redesigned to function effectively in the changed environment. The next three years proved to be tough ones indeed for Fidel.

"More Fantasies than Food"

"For over three years, the Castro regime has fed its people more fantasies than food," wrote historian Theodore Draper in 1964.[107] And in truth Fidel's infant government promised much more than it delivered. The Sierra fighting began to pale in the light of the newer, greater battle that raged against a failed economy.

On the plus side, Fidel knew that the economy ranked a distant second in the revolutionary order of march—at least in the early going. Nature had richly endowed the island itself. With the added help of the Soviet bloc, Fidel never doubted his ability to navigate through the choppy waters of social change. Nor did it hurt that his government ruled with a weighted hand. Because Fidel—*el líder máximo*—ruled supremely, Cuba's economy became in fact whatever Fidel said it was on whatever day he said it. In fairness, he tried hard to give the people a better life.

From his harried hopes of "Agrarian Reform" to his dented dream of a "Ten-Million Ton [Sugar] Harvest," Fidel has suffered one failure after another on the home front.

On July 1963, Fidel complained, "Everybody is a volunteer in the front rank demanding things, but everybody hangs back when it comes to producing."[108] He needed new solutions to old problems.

The Castro Government

In a quote from Fred Ward's Inside Cuba Today, *Fidel explains the structure and workings of Cuba's government.*

"The highest political responsibilities are in the hands of the Central Committee of the Communist Party. The Constitution itself recognizes the leading role of the Party. The Party lays down the political line, and it is supposed that the state, through the National Assembly, will carry out that program. If that did not happen, the Party would be discredited, and there would be a political crisis."

Although Castro vowed to make Cuba less dependent on sugar cane, which he harvests in this photo, the economy remained dependent upon the cash crop.

He then viewed the sugar harvest—or *zafra*—as a military operation and organized "brigades" to bring it in. On many occasions, Fidel entered the cane fields himself. Armed with a machete, he joined the people's battle for a better sugar-based economy. In 1970, his tactics produced a record 8.5-million-ton harvest. But even this record yield failed to make up for losses in other parts of the economy. He next turned to cows.

Fidel attempted to develop a super breed of cow—a blend of Cébu and Holstein. He hoped to establish himself in the eyes of science and the world as the new "Father of Genetics." At the same time, he meant to create a cattle-based economy (or at least to supplement his sugar base). The nature of the cows, however, didn't allow for cross-breeding, and the experiment failed.

Still, with the aid of sweat, tears, fears, and the communist bloc countries—the USSR, China and others—Fidel's revolution moved forward. And not everything resulted in failure.

After a decade of revolution, Herbert L. Matthews wrote:

> Only the most stubborn and emotional critics of the Castro regime would argue that the Cuban peasants, taken as a whole and considering "fringe benefits" in food, medical care, education, and housing, are not better off today than ever before.[109]

Chapter
7 Crises in the Caribbean: Pigs, Missiles, and "Little Wars"

The first decade of the revolution demanded much more of Fidel's government than simply making a better life for the peasants. A great many Cubans opposed Fidel and his vision of Cuba's future. Nor was the United States—that "monster in the north"—pleased about having a communist nation located ninety miles off Key West, Florida. Something, they all agreed, had to be done. An attempt to bring about that *something* entered the history books at a place called Bahía de Cochinos—the Bay of Pigs.

A military move designed to counter a revolt against civil authority is called a counterinsurgency. Robert Kennedy once defined it as "social reform under pressure."[110] His simple phrase hardly suggests the dangers involved in such operations. It was a new kind of warfare. The task fell to Robert's brother John not to define it, but, rather, to test its limits.

The plan originated under President Eisenhower. But its execution carried over to his successor, President John F. Kennedy. It called for the invasion of Cuba and overthrow of Fidel Castro's government by expatriate Cubans. A government more in keeping with U.S. interests would then be installed in its place. In spite of grave doubts, President Kennedy elected to proceed with the operation. He lived to regret his decision and later asked his special counsel Theodore C. Sorensen, "How could I have been so stupid [as] to let them go ahead?"[111]

Under the direction of the CIA, the training of Cuban exiles began in Guatemala and Nicaragua by late 1959. The Cuban expatriots took the name of Brigade 2506, the serial number of the first volunteer to die in training.

On Saturday, April 15, 1961—well over a year later—six B-26 medium bombers of the brigade struck three Cuban airfields.

John F. Kennedy planned to use Cuban expatriates to invade and overthrow Castro's government.

Striking at the same time, two planes attacked at each of the three sites of Havana, San Antonio, and Santiago. Reportedly, the raiders completely destroyed Fidel's air force. In reality, the attacks left four British-made Sea Fury light attack bombers, one B-26, and two T-33 jet trainers. The remaining aircraft would soon prove critical to the outcome of the Bay of Pigs invasion.

Historian Theodore Draper later wrote of the operation: "The ill-fated invasion of Cuba in April, 1961, was one of those rare politico-military events—a perfect failure."[112]

At Colón Cemetery the next day, during a speech given at a funeral service for seven bombing victims, Fidel compared the air attack with Pearl Harbor. But he declared that it was "twice as treacherous and a thousand times more cowardly."[113] He warned the crowd of about ten thousand angry (at the United States) people of further offensive acts to come from paid U.S. mercenaries.

Continuing, he explained, "The United States sponsored the attack because it cannot forgive us for achieving a Socialist revolution under their noses."[114] It marked the first time that Fidel described the revolution as "Socialist" (read "Communist").

The Bay of Pigs Invasion

On Monday, April 17, at 1:15 A.M., approximately fifteen hundred men of the Brigade 2506 invasion force started ashore in the Bay of Pigs. They landed first on Playa Larga ("Red Beach") and then on Playa Girón ("Blue Beach"). Under the

Cuban exiles train in the Caribbean in 1961 in preparation to execute the Bay of Pigs invasion.

command of José "Pepe" San Roman, the mission of the American-trained and -equipped invaders was to execute a simple plan, as described by Herbert L. Matthews in his book *Fidel Castro:*

Playa Girón is a horseshoe-shaped beach about a mile wide. For about 100 yards the water is quite shallow; then it shelves suddenly and steeply. Ships can come close to shore and men can get out and wade onto land. Along the beach and close to the water, across to Playa Larga, is an excellent paved road running east and west. From there the only road goes due north. A small but adequate airfield was just across the road from Playa Girón.

The idea was to establish a beachhead that should have been easy to defend because there were only those two roads at right angles and swamp all around. The defenders could come down only on the north-south road to Playa Larga. If the beachhead had been established, the Americans could have flown in the pseudo-government [a false government of Cuban exiles] they had formed, which [then] would have asked for recognition and help.[115]

Because of a series of errors in both planning and execution, the battle plan failed with a capital *F*. Reduced to a single factor, the failure stemmed from the ability of Fidel's few remaining aircraft to control the skies over the battle scene. They were able to operate without opposition against troops on land and ships at sea.

Earlier, the CIA planning had relied heavily on a mass uprising of Cuban citizens once the invasion began. That didn't happen. Nor did the invaders receive any land, sea, or air support from the Americans as they had expected. With control of the air, Fidel's forces halted the advance of brigade troops barely beyond the beaches. Sea Furies and T-33 jets sank the

freighter *Rio Escondido* offshore. They forced another freighter, the *Houston*, aground, about five miles south of the landing beaches. Most of the brigade's ammunition was lost with the two freighters. Still another brigade vessel, the infantry landing ship *J. Barbara*, fled to the open sea.

Brigade paratroopers jumped short of their target zone and were unable to block the north-south road to the battle area. Fidel's large army rushed to the scene with commanding tanks and artillery. The brigade's fight for Cuba's so-called liberation—the fight that failed—ended at 5:30 P.M., on April 19, 1961.

An immensely happy Fidel announced over the radio: "The invaders have been annihilated. The revolution has emerged victorious. It destroyed in less than seventy-two hours the army organized during many months by the imperialistic Government of the United States."[116]

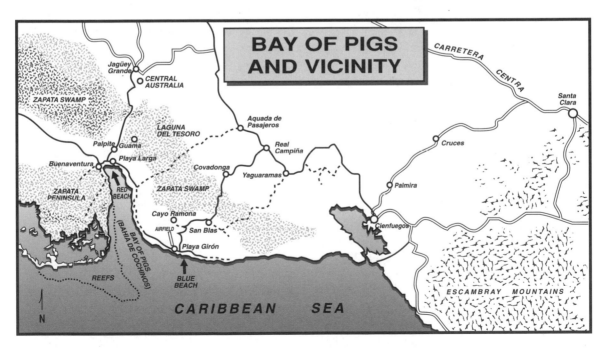

A remnant of a U.S. B-26 bomber used by U.S.-supported Cuban exiles is a testimony to the failure of the Bay of Pigs invasion. The invasion cemented Castro's popularity with both communist and non-communist nations that disliked the United States.

The brigade suffered losses of 107 dead; 1,189 were taken prisoner. Fidel's losses numbered 161 dead. But he had taken on the hated "Colossus to the North," and he had won.

The sorry affair at the Bay of Pigs set the tone of future relations between Cuba and the United States for years to come. It also strengthened Cuba's ties with the USSR.

In a note to President Kennedy on April 18, Premier Khrushchev wrote: "We will extend to the Cuban people and their government all the necessary aid to repulse the armed attack. We are sincerely interested in the relaxation of international tension, but if others aggravate it, then we shall reply in full measure."[117]

Kennedy answered with strong words of his own: "In the event of any military intervention by outside forces, we will immediately honor our obligations under the inter-American system to protect the hemisphere against external aggression."[118]

Eighteen months later, Khrushchev called Kennedy's bluff and backed his words with missiles.

Nuclear Missiles Discovered in Cuba

In a televised report to the nation on October 22, 1962, President Kennedy revealed that U.S. surveillance (mainly photographs taken by U-2 spy planes) had "established the fact that a series of offensive missile sites is now in preparation in Cuba."[119] He indicated that the sites posed a threat to most of the major cities in the Western Hemisphere. He further disclosed that jet bombers capable of delivering nuclear weapons were being uncrated there.

Kennedy told the American public that a naval and air quarantine of the island had already been ordered. It would not be lifted, he told them, until all offensive weapons were dismantled and removed from Cuba under United Nations supervision.

Furthermore, the launching of any nuclear missile from Cuba against any Western Hemisphere nation, he warned, would be considered an attack on the United States "requiring a full retaliatory attack on the Soviet Union."[120] The president then placed U.S. forces on alert. Preparations commenced immediately for an "if necessary" invasion of Cuba.

The Soviet government responded to President Kennedy's message in kind the next day. It alerted its armed forces and challenged the right of the United States

Khrushchev used the Bay of Pigs invasion as a launching point to try to covertly plant Soviet missiles in Cuba. Here, aerial photos taken by U.S. surveillance aircraft show a surface-to-air missile assembly depot in Cuba.

Under U.S. surveillance, a Soviet freighter begins the removal of Soviet missiles from Cuba, ending the immediate threat of nuclear war between the two superpowers.

to quarantine its shipments to Cuba. The United States proceeded with its invasion preparations.

At this point, the world entered into eight terror-filled days of terrible anxiety, as it moved closer to a nuclear war than ever before or since. Over the next six days (October 24-29), the world's two superpowers stood nose-to-nose, eyeball-to-eyeball, while, together, the rest of the world held its breath.

When push came to stronger push, Fidel—not surprisingly, but much to his displeasure—became a minor actor on a crowded stage. He found himself completely left out of the power talks and decision-making processes between the United States and the USSR.

Nuclear Chaos Averted

On October 29, after an exchange of letters between President Kennedy and Premier Khrushchev, the Soviet leader backed down. Khrushchev agreed to stop construction of missile bases in Cuba, and

to dismantle and remove his missiles there under UN supervision. In return, Kennedy agreed to lift his quarantine and vowed not to invade Cuba. To the relief of all humankind, the "crisis in the Caribbean" ended quietly.

But whose idea was it to put missiles in Cuba in defiance of the U.S. Monroe Doctrine? What was to be gained by such a foolish and dangerous willingness to risk nuclear destruction? As is true of most events of this stature, the responsibility or blame must be shared by all three of the involved nations. For example, the U.S. policy toward the Castro government did little to lessen Fidel's fear of his northern neighbor.

"The Cuba Project," a National Security Council report issued on November 30, 1961, set forth its intentions toward Fidel: "The United States will help the people of Cuba overthrow the Communist regime within Cuba and institute a new government with which the United States can live in peace."[121]

Even now, the issue remains unclear as to whose idea it was to install nuclear missiles in Cuba. Fidel afterward told a French reporter:

The only thing we asked the Russians to do was to make clear to the U.S. that an attack on us was an attack on the Soviet Union. We had an extensive discussion before arriving at the proposal of installing guided missiles, a proposal which *surprised us at first and gave us great pause* [Castro's emphasis]. We finally went along with the Soviet proposal because, on the one hand, the Russians convinced us that the U.S. would not let itself be [frightened off] by [regular] weapons and secondly because it was impossible for us not to share the risks which the Soviet Union was taking to save us.[122]

Nikita Khrushchev told a different story. In Moscow, to the visiting U.S. secretary of the interior Stuart Udall, Khrushchev said:

Now, as to Cuba—here is an area that could really lead to some unexpected circumstances. [Castro] hasn't much modern military equipment, *so he asked us to supply some* [emphasis added]. But only for defense. However, if you attack Cuba, that would create an entirely different situation.[123]

Whether Fidel or Nikita first suggested installing missiles in Cuba begs the real issue: The presence of the missiles there brought the world to the very edge of eternity. And the degree of guilt or innocence assigned to each involved nation fades in importance in the light of a nuclear blast.

Secretary of State Dean Rusk said of the Cuban missile crisis: "We were eyeball to eyeball, and I think the other fellow blinked."[124] How fortunate for humankind.

Risking Nuclear Destruction

Tad Szulc, author of Fidel: A Critical Portrait, *interviewed Fidel twenty-five years after the missile crisis. Fidel Castro explained to him the reasoning behind the decision to install Soviet nuclear missiles in Cuba.*

"We preferred the risks of great tension, whatever they were, of great crisis to the risks of the [inability to act], of waiting [without being able to act] for a United States invasion of Cuba. At least they [the missiles] gave us a nuclear umbrella, and we felt much more satisfied with the response we were giving to the policy of hostility and aggression toward our country. From a strictly moral as well as strictly legal viewpoint, as a sovereign country we had the right to make use of the type of arms we considered gave us a guarantee. And in the same way that the United States had missiles in Italy and Turkey, and in the same way the United States had bases in all parts of the world around the Soviet Union."

In the aftermath of one of the world's darkest moments, Nikita Khrushchev lost favor in the USSR and was soon replaced as premier. Little more than a year later, John Kennedy fell victim to an assassin's bullets. But Fidel came through the grim episode stronger than ever. As the leader of a tiny nation, he had captured international attention. He could now direct his efforts toward sharing his revolution with the rest of the world.

"Little Wars"

In contrast to his economic shortcomings, Fidel excels at breathing new life into guerrilla—or "little war"—tactics. He welcomes any opportunity to spread them about the globe.

Journalist Georgie Anne Geyer describes his unique abilities well: "Militarize! Mobilize! Demonize!—those were Castro's talents, not bottling beer or selling sewing machines or preparing proposals for the World Bank."[125] To those ends, Fidel trains a minimum of fifteen hundred *guerrilleros*—"little fighters"—a year.

Over the years, Fidel has built one of the largest and most powerful military forces of all the Third World countries in the Western Hemisphere. During this time, the United States has concentrated on long-range economic development programs such as the Alliance for Progress. Fidel directly opposes every American effort by exporting his revolutionary machinery to each country in which the United States initiates a program. He seems to draw a great sense of power and satisfaction from his ability to undermine the best-laid U.S. plans.

Fidel has expanded his influence by supporting leftist governments already in place, sending troops to such places as Angola, Mozambique, and Nicaragua. And he has attempted to overthrow opposition governments by training guerrillas and using them to infiltrate Latin American countries, as in the cases of Peru, Venezuela, Bolivia, Guatemala, El Salvador, and Colombia.

His guerrilla attacks began as early as April 1959, when some eighty of his men sailed from Cuba to "liberate" Panama in a plan that quickly failed.

On October 8, 1967, Che Guevara met a violent death in the Bolivian jungle. One of the true heroes of the revolution, Che was killed while leading another such venture. Questions arising from his death remain unanswered. Che left Cuba in 1965 because, in his words, "other nations in the world call for my modest efforts."[125] Some believe instead that he left Cuba because of a falling-out with Fidel. Che led another guerrilla movement in the Congo

Cuban troops in 1988. With the help of his military, Castro attempted to aid other revolutions worldwide.

Fidel's Account of Che's Death

According to Fidel, Che Guevara didn't die in battle but was murdered while a prisoner of Bolivian soldiers. Fidel is quoted in K.S. Karol's book Guerrillas in Power *as having said:*

"Major Miguel Ayoroa and Colonel Andrés Selnich, two [Bolivian] Rangers trained by the Americans, ordered a noncommissioned officer, Mario Terán, to murder Che. Terán went in [a schoolhouse where Che was being held] completely drunk, and Che, who had heard the shots that had just killed a Bolivian and a Peruvian fighter, seeing the brute hesitate, said to him firmly: 'Shoot, don't be afraid.' Terán left the room; and his superiors, Ayoroa and Selnich, had to repeat the order, which he finally carried out, firing his machine gun at Che from the waist down. The official tale that Che had died a few hours after combat was already in circulation; this was why the executioners gave orders not to shoot him in the neck or head so as not to produce instantly fatal wounds. Che's agony was thus cruelly prolonged till a sergeant, who was also drunk, finally killed him with a pistol shot in the left side."

that ended in failure after a few months. He returned to Cuba only briefly before moving on again, this time to Bolivia.

Some stories persist that Che was becoming a threat to Fidel and his dealings with the Soviets. Did Fidel send Che to be killed in the Bolivian jungle as some suggest? Or did Che act on his own? Fidel chooses not to shed light on these circumstances. After Che's death, however, Fidel's relations with the Soviets clearly did improve.

By the end of the 1980s—despite the embarrassing defeat of an ill-prepared group of Cuban soldiers by the United States-Caribbean Security Forces on Grenada in 1983—Fidel stood solidly in place as Cuba's *líder máximo*. And he was still changing history.

Che Guevara died in the Bolivian jungle leading guerrilla forces in 1967. Some have questioned whether Castro had a role in his death.

8 Cuba Today: Faded Dreams

As this is written, Fidel Castro still stands tall at the head of government in Cuba—a year and four decades after Moncada. But where now stands the revolution of his making? What has become of its promise of independence and a share of the good life for every Cuban? Are the Cuban people better off today than they were before Fidel's great experiment? Has the revolution been worth the pain, suffering, and sacrifices that it has leveled on millions of Cubans? Fidel thinks so:

> If I were to have the privilege of living my life over again, I would do many things differently from the way I have done them up to now; but at the same time I can assure you that I would fight all my life with the same passion for the same objectives I have fought for up to now. COUNTRY OR DEATH—WE SHALL OVERCOME.[127]

Nothing coming out of Cuba recently suggests that he might have changed his outlook. Nor do reports from Havana indicate that he's willing to step down as Cuba's maximum leader any time soon. Quite the opposite. In February 1993, he was "elected" to a new five-year term as president of the Council of State.

Cubans demonstrate in support of Castro in 1992. Despite the hardships many Cubans face, most remain loyal to the controversial leader.

The Soviet Union's long financial support of Cuba ended when the USSR collapsed in 1989. Here, students topple a statue of Lenin following communism's demise.

Fidel steered Cuba toward communism in the early 1960s. Since then, both Cuba's economy and its military have leaned heavily on "Mother Russia" for help. Many Fidel-watchers think that the breakup of the Soviet Union will soon spell the end of Fidel and his regime. Other observers of Fidel predict that his ability to adapt to change in an ever-changing world will see him through tougher times yet. And if the choice is left to Fidel, they believe that he will elect to remain in office until he dies.

Life in Cuba

How does this affect the average Cuban? What is life like under Fidel in Cuba today? After a recent visit to Cuba, historian Robert E. Quirk described the current lifestyle there:

> There seemed to be no end to the crises in Cuba. Lights were going out in the cities. More factories closed. Others operated only during the day. Bus routes were cut. The country was running out of gasoline, of paper, of new clothing, of vital foodstuffs. Children over seven were no longer guar-

anteed milk. Black markets flourished, and everyone tried to get illegal dollars. A woman in Havana told Jo Thomas, a correspondent for the *New York Times*, that her family had had no meat for over a month. Another woman remarked bitterly that "it might have been different with Ochoa."[128]

Gen. Arnaldo Ochoa Sánchez was a hero of the revolution who had fought with honor in Angola and Ethiopia. Fidel himself had proclaimed the general an "exceptional warrior of the fatherland."[129] In April 1989, rumors whispered in Havana told of certain high-ranking military

Just as in the economically troubled Soviet Union, Cuban citizens wait in lines to buy milk in 1991. Castro's promised prosperity for all citizens has yet to materialize.

officers forming together in growing opposition to Fidel. Ochoa was arrested in June and tried on charges of "corruption." On July 13, 1989, he met death with honor in front of a firing squad.

Cuban general Rafael del Pino, who had fled Cuba earlier, said of Ochoa:

He had already lost all confidence in the Revolution . . . and he criticized the Revolution. That was unforgivable. I was inside that hell and I know how the devil works. [Echoes of José Martí.] Ochoa had to pay for two things: He was too dangerous for Fidel, and he was the only one to have the prestige and the love of the Armed Forces.[130]

Once again, apparently, Fidel had shown himself capable of doing whatever it took to remain in power.

Keeping On with the Revolution

When the wellspring of Soviet aid slowed down to a trickle, Fidel looked to fellow Third World countries for help. In the summer of 1991, he flew off to Mexico's vacation island of Cozumel. There, so close to where his revolution began, he met with the presidents of Colombia, Mexico, and Venezuela. His appeal for oil, trade, and tourists brought him sympathy but little else. Cubans sighed and drew their stomachs tighter yet.

In June 1992, Fidel invited a large group of businessmen to Havana—most of them Americans—to discuss investment opportunities in Cuba. Talks went well until the businessmen asked Fidel whether

he planned to initiate "democratic reforms." Fidel told them in effect that Cuba already had democracy. He wasn't interested in making Cuba more like the United States. He pointed to internal problems in the United States.

Right then, he told them, U.S. military forces were being used to "invade" Los Angeles, a city torn by riots. "And you ask me about democracy?" he said.[131]

Nothing accomplished, the businessmen left.

Although Fidel hails forth as maximum leader, in truth, it is King Sugar that rules over Cuba, and with the loss of Soviet aid, this is true now more than ever. But year after year, Cuba's sugar crop has failed to produce Fidel's cherished "Ten-Million-Ton Harvest." As the sugar harvest shrinks, so, too, does the Cuban stomach.

So, after all these years under Fidel, what do his people *really* think about what his revolution has done for them? Under Batista, Cubans enjoyed the highest living standard of all Latin American countries. In many ways their lifestyles resembled those of the United States. Would they like to return to those days?

Robert Quirk's book *Fidel Castro* offers keen insight into the question:

Imitate the United States? Why? asked the Cubans. True, they wanted political freedoms and a decent standard of living. But their country had no drug problems. No gangs in the cities. No race riots. In the evening young blacks played dominoes under dim street lights. A mixed-race dance group performed Afro-Cuban rhumbas in a [rundown] meeting house. The people had never asked to be communists. Nor had they wanted to link their des-

A Medal for Fidel?

According to Georgie Anne Geyer in Guerrilla Prince, *Alina Revuelta, Fidel's daughter by Naty Revuelta, has openly attacked her father in the press.*

"He deserves a medal for destroying Cuba," she told one reporter. In another interview, she said, "This man is crazy, and everything is going to end in a bloodbath, because the government is still prepared to last many years. They are always inventing some motive in order to make the Cuban people think about other things that are not the reality. It is all like a novel that you read until you suddenly open your eyes unless you die."

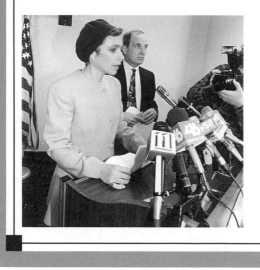

Fidel's daughter, Alina Revuelta, talks to the press. She has openly criticized her famous father.

tinies to those of the Soviet Union. That had been Castro's doings. Now outsiders were asking them to trade in their lives for an American future.[132]

When a reporter for the *New York Times* spoke with a Cuban worker in Holguín, a city in eastern Cuba, Quirk continues, the worker said, "I can walk the streets at night without fear of anyone." "If you ask me which country I would rather live in, yours or mine, the answer will always be mine."[133] Life in Cuba goes on.

Meanwhile, the fundamental question as to the success or failure of the Cuban Revolution must remain, of necessity, unanswered. For now, however, it seems fair to say that, under Fidel, the eternal hope of all Cubans for a *Cuba Libre*—a free Cuba—remains still a dream . . . and a faded one at best.

Notes

Introduction: Born to Change History

1. Quoted in Carlos Franqui, *Diary of the Cuban Revolution*. New York: The Viking Press, 1980.

2. Theodore Draper, *Castroism: Theory and Practice*. New York: Frederick A. Praeger, Inc., 1965.

Chapter 1: Moncada: The Birth of the 26th of July Movement

3. Herbert L. Matthews, *Fidel Castro*. New York: Simon and Schuster, 1969.

4. Georgie Anne Geyer, *Guerrilla Prince: The Untold Story of Fidel Castro*. Kansas City, MO: Andrews and McMeel, 1993.

5. Geyer, *Guerrilla Prince*.

6. Quoted in Geyer, *Guerrilla Prince*.

7. Quoted in Geyer, *Guerrilla Prince*.

8. Quoted in Geyer, *Guerrilla Prince*.

9. Quoted in Geyer, *Guerrilla Prince*.

10. Quoted in Geyer, *Guerrilla Prince*.

11. Tad Szulc, *Fidel: A Critical Portrait*. New York: William Morrow and Company, Inc., 1986.

12. Szulc, *Fidel*.

13. Hugh Thomas, *The Cuban Revolution*. New York: Harper & Row Publishers, Inc., 1977.

14. Geyer, *Guerrilla Prince*.

15. Szulc, *Fidel*.

16. Quoted in Franqui, *Diary of the Cuban Revolution*.

17. Quoted in Franqui, *Diary of the Cuban Revolution*.

18. Quoted in Franqui, *Diary of the Cuban Revolution*.

19. Quoted in Geyer, *Guerrilla Prince*.

Chapter 2: Cuba Before the Revolution: The Long Pursuit of Freedom

20. Saul K. Padover, *The Complete Jefferson*. New York: Tudor Publishing Company, 1943.

21. Henry Adams, ed., *The Writings of Albert Gallatin*, Vol. I. New York: Antiquarian Press, Ltd., 1960.

22. Quoted in *Bartlett's Familiar Quotations*, 16th ed.

23. Michael J. Mazarr, *Semper Fidel: America & Cuba 1776–1988*. Baltimore: The Nautical & Aviation Publishing Company of America, Inc., 1988.

24. Mazarr, *Semper Fidel*.

25. José Martí, Letter to Manuel Mercado, 1895. Quoted in *Bartlett's Familiar Quotations*, 16th ed.

26. Boris Goldenberg, *The Cuban Revolution and Latin America*. New York: Frederick A. Praeger, Inc., 1965.

27. Matthews, *Fidel Castro*.

28. Matthews, *Fidel Castro*.

29. Quoted in Mazarr, *Semper Fidel*.

Chapter 3: Castro: Man of Destiny

30. Quoted in Szulc, *Fidel*.

31. Quoted in Szulc, *Fidel*.

32. Quoted in Franqui, *Diary of the Cuban Revolution*.

33. Robert E. Quirk, *Fidel Castro*. New York: W.W. Norton & Company, Inc. 1993.

34. Quoted in Franqui, *Diary of the Cuban Revolution*.

35. Quoted in Franqui, *Diary of the Cuban Revolution*.

36. Quoted in Franqui, *Diary of the Cuban Revolution*.

37. Quoted in Franqui, *Diary of the Cuban Revolution.*

38. Quoted in Franqui, *Diary of the Cuban Revolution.*

39. Quoted in Franqui, *Diary of the Cuban Revolution.*

40. Quoted in Szulc, *Fidel.*

41. Quoted in Franqui, *Diary of the Cuban Revolution.*

42. Quoted in Matthews, *Fidel Castro.*

43. Quoted in Franqui, *Diary of the Cuban Revolution.*

44. Quoted in Geyer, *Guerrilla Prince.*

45. Quoted in Geyer, *Guerrilla Prince.*

46. Quoted in Geyer, *Guerrilla Prince.*

47. Quoted in Franqui, *Diary of the Cuban Revolution.*

48. Quoted in Franqui, *Diary of the Cuban Revolution.*

49. Szulc, *Fidel.*

Chapter 4: M-26 in Mexico: The Preparation

50. Quoted in Geyer, *Guerrilla Prince.*

51. Quoted in Szulc, *Fidel.*

52. Quoted in Szulc, *Fidel.*

53. Quoted in Matthews, *Fidel Castro.*

54. Quoted in Geyer, *Guerrilla Prince.*

55. Quoted in Geyer, *Guerrilla Prince.*

56. Quoted in Geyer, *Guerrilla Prince.*

57. Quoted in Szulc, *Fidel.*

58. Quoted in Szulc, *Fidel.*

59. Quoted in Matthews, *Fidel Castro.*

60. Quoted in Geyer, *Guerrilla Prince.*

61. Quoted in Franqui, *Diary of the Cuban Revolution.*

Chapter 5: The Sierra Maestra: The Fight

62. Quoted in Franqui, *Diary of the Cuban Revolution.*

63. Quoted in Franqui, *Diary of the Cuban Revolution.*

64. Quoted in Franqui, *Diary of the Cuban Revolution.*

65. Quoted in Szulc, *Fidel.*

66. Quoted in Geyer, *Guerrilla Prince.*

67. Quoted in Geyer, *Guerrilla Prince.*

68. Quoted in Franqui, *Diary of the Cuban Revolution.*

69. Quoted in Geyer, *Guerrilla Prince.*

70. Quoted in Szulc, *Fidel.*

71. Matthews, *Fidel Castro.*

72. Matthews, *Fidel Castro.*

73. Matthews, *Fidel Castro.*

74. Quoted in Franqui, *Diary of the Cuban Revolution.*

75. Quoted in Franqui, *Diary of the Cuban Revolution.*

76. Quoted in Geyer, *Guerrilla Prince.*

77. Quoted in Matthews, *Fidel Castro.*

78. Quoted in Szulc, *Fidel.*

79. Quoted in Geyer, *Guerrilla Prince.*

80. Quoted in Szulc, *Fidel.*

81. Quoted in Szulc, *Fidel.*

82. Quoted in Geyer, *Guerrilla Prince.*

83. Quoted in Quirk, *Fidel Castro.*

84. Quoted in Szulc, *Fidel.*

Chapter 6: Rebels in Havana: The Revolution

85. Franqui, *Diary of the Cuban Revolution.*

86. Quoted in Geyer, *Guerrilla Prince.*

87. Ruby Hart Phillips, *Cuba: Island of Paradox.* New York: McDowell, Obolensky, 1960.

88. Quoted in Geyer, *Guerrilla Prince.*

89. Quoted in Geyer, *Guerrilla Prince.*

90. Quoted in Szulc, *Fidel.*

91. Quoted in Quirk, *Fidel Castro.*

92. Quoted in Quirk, *Fidel Castro.*

93. Quoted in Louis A. Pérez Jr., *Cuba:*

Between Reform and Revolution. New York: Oxford University Press, Inc., 1988.

94. Quoted in Matthews, *Fidel Castro.*

95. Quoted in Szulc, *Fidel.*

96. Quoted in Geyer, *Guerrilla Prince.*

97. Quoted in Geyer, *Guerrilla Prince.*

98. Quoted in Geyer, *Guerrilla Prince.*

99. Quoted in Szulc, *Fidel.*

100. Quoted in Szulc, *Fidel.*

101. Quoted in Quirk, *Fidel Castro.*

102. Quoted in Quirk, *Fidel Castro.*

103. Quoted in Thomas, *The Cuban Revolution.*

104. Quoted in Geyer, *Guerrilla Prince.*

105. Quoted in Geyer, *Guerrilla Prince.*

106. Quoted in Szulc, *Fidel.*

107. Theodore Draper, article in *The New Leader,* April 13, 1964.

108. Matthews, *Fidel Castro.*

109. Matthews, *Fidel Castro.*

Chapter 7: Crises in the Caribbean: Pigs, Missiles, and "Little Wars"

110. Quoted in Geyer, *Guerrilla Prince.*

111. Quoted in Peter Wyden, *Bay of Pigs: The Untold Story.* New York: Simon and Schuster, 1979.

112. Theodore Draper, *Castro's Revolution: Myths and Realities.* New York: Frederick A. Praeger, Inc., 1962.

113. Szulc, *Fidel.*

114. Wyden, *Bay of Pigs.*

115. Matthews, *Fidel Castro.*

116. Matthews, *Fidel Castro.*

117. Quoted in Quirk, *Fidel Castro.*

118. Quoted in Quirk, *Fidel Castro.*

119. Quoted in R. Ernest Dupuy and Trevor N. Dupuy, *The Encyclopedia of Military History.* New York: Harper & Row, Publishers, 1977.

120. Quoted in Dupuy and Dupuy, *The Encyclopedia of Military History.*

121. Quoted in Robert Smith Thompson, *The Missiles of October: The Declassified Story of John F. Kennedy and the Cuban Missile Crisis.* New York: Simon and Schuster, 1992.

122. Quoted in Thompson, *The Missiles of October.*

123. Quoted in Thompson, *The Missiles of October.*

124. Quoted in Dino A. Brugioni, *Eyeball to Eyeball: The Inside Story of the Cuban Missile Crisis.* New York: Random House, 1991.

125. Quoted in Geyer, *Guerrilla Prince.*

126. Quoted in K.S. Karol, *Guerrillas in Power.* New York: Hill & Wang, 1970.

Chapter 8: Cuba Today: Faded Dreams

127. Quoted in Fred Ward, *Inside Cuba Today.* New York: Crown Publishers, Inc., 1978.

128. Quirk, *Fidel Castro.*

129. Quoted in Quirk, *Fidel Castro.*

130. Quoted in Geyer, *Guerrilla Prince.*

131. Quoted in Quirk, *Fidel Castro.*

132. Quirk, *Fidel Castro.*

133. Quoted in Quirk, *Fidel Castro.*

Glossary

Acción Revolucionaria Oriente (ANR): political action group in Oriente province headed by Frank País.

amnesty: a general pardon, especially for offenses against a country.

Antilles: the West Indies, excluding the Bahamas: the Greater and Lesser Antilles.

assassin: one who kills by violent means, usually from religious or political motives.

Auténtico Party: Cuban conservative political party claiming to represent the ideals of José Martí.

barbudos: bearded guerrillas.

Batistiano: loyal follower of Batista.

Bogotazo: riotous event in Bogotá, Colombia, in April 1948, after the assassination of political leader Jorge Eliecer Gaitán.

capitalism: an economic system in which trade and industry is controlled by private owners.

caudillo: leader, especially a political boss.

clandestine: kept or done in secret.

colonialism: the policy of acquiring or maintaining colonies.

"Colossus to the North": José Martí's phrase for the United States.

communism: a political movement seeking to overthrow capitalism and establish a social system in which property is owned by the community and each member works for the common good.

conquistador: one who conquers, especially the Spanish conquerors.

counterinsurgency: action taken to counter rebellious activities.

¡Cuba Libre!: Free Cuba!; a revolutionary battle cry.

el líder máximo: the maximum leader.

exile: being sent away from one's home country as a form of punishment; one who is sent away.

Federación Estudiantil Universitaria (FEU): powerful students' organization at the University of Havana.

Fidelista: follower of Fidel Castro.

finca: country house, estate; ranch, farm.

fusillade: the firing of guns together or continuously.

Gallego: native of Galicia province, Spain.

garrison: troops stationed in a town or fort to defend it; the fort or building they occupy.

gringo: a foreigner in Spain or Latin America, especially when British or American; often used to demean.

guerrilla: one who engages in irregular warfare, usually acting independently and in small groups.

guerrillero: literally "little guerrilla"; name given to Cuban patriots who fought against Spanish conquerors.

haves and have-nots: the very rich and the very poor.

imperialism: the desire to acquire colonies and dependencies.

Insurrectional Revolutionary Union (UIR): Organization of Cuban political activists.

la fruta madura: Cuban name for what wealthy slaveowners considered to be the U.S. policy toward Cuba: preserving the fruit (Cuba) on the Spanish vine; when the fruit ripened, it would fall into the U.S. lap; that is, the United States would take possession of Cuba without having to fight Spain.

las masas: the crowd, often used by Fidel to denote "the people."

llano: lowlands, the name given to the urban branch of the revolutionaries.

Los Doce: The Twelve, said by Fidel Castro to be all that was left of his *Granma* invading force after its first encounter with Batista soldiers; the core group of the guerrilla army.

manipulation: Something cleverly or craftily arranged or influenced.

Marist: member of the Roman Catholic Society of Mary devoted to education.

Moncada: military barracks (or fort) in Santiago; site of Fidel Castro's first armed attack against the Batista regime on July 26, 1953; birthplace of the 26th of July Movement.

Monroe Doctrine: a U.S. policy that effectively told Europe to keep "hands off" of the Americas.

oppression: an act of harsh governing; treatment marked by continual cruelty or injustice.

Oriente: easternmost province of Cuba; province of Fidel Castro's birth and boyhood.

Ortodoxo Party: Cuban radical, reformist political party.

National Directorate: loose assemblage of revolutionary leadership that attempted to unify rebel activities throughout the island, for the most part ignored by Fidel; not to be confused with the Revolutionary Directorate.

padrino: godfather.

Platt Amendment: agreement signed by the United States and Cuba after the Spanish-American War (Cuban Second War for Independence) that allowed U.S. intervention in Cuba when U.S. interests were threatened; the agreement was revoked in 1934.

propaganda: publicity that spreads information or ideas intended to persuade or convince people.

psychological warfare: actions or propaganda designed to weaken an enemy's morale.

quarantine: a state of enforced isolation.

rebellion: open resistance to authority, especially armed resistance to an established government.

regime: a method or system of government or administration.

repression: the act of keeping down or suppressing.

Revolt of the Sergeants: 1933 revolt of Cuban army noncommissioned officers against U.S.-sponsored Céspedes government; the revolt was led by Fulgencio Batista.

revolution: substitution of a new system of government, usually by force.

revolutionary: of political revolution; a person who supports or takes part in a political revolution.

Revolutionary Directorate (DR): group of politically active students headed by José Antonio Echeverría.

Santiago: capital of Oriente province.

Siboney Beach: beach outside Santiago, named for Ciboney Indians, early inhabitants of the island; famous as a tourist attraction.

sierra: mountain, the name given to the mountain branch of the revolutionaries.

Sierra Cristal: mountain range northeast of Sierra Maestra in Oriente province; scene of second front opened by Raúl Castro.

Sierra Maestra: Cuba's highest mountain range; located in Oriente province, the range provided a base from which the *Fidelistas* conducted their guerrilla warfare.

Socialist Revolutionary Movement (MSR): organization of Cuban political activists.

strategy: the planning and directing of an entire operation of a campaign or war, as distinguished from tactics.

surveillance: close observation.

tactics: the art of placing or moving forces skillfully in battle, as distinguished from strategy.

tyranny: oppressive use of power.

zafra: sugar-making season; sugar harvest.

For Further Reading

Ernesto Betancourt, *Cuban Leadership After Castro*. Miami: Research Institute, University of Miami, 1988. This book is written by a Cuban economist and offers an informed look at what the future may hold for Cuba beyond Castro.

Peter G. Bourne, *Fidel*. New York: Dodd, Mead, & Company, 1986. A lesser-known biography, this book provides a contrasting view of the Cuban leader when compared with earlier and later works.

Terence Cannon, *Revolutionary Cuba*. New York: Thomas Y. Crowell, 1981. This account details what life was like in Cuba two decades after the revolution. Much of Cannon's portrayal of Cuban life remains valid today.

Jules Dubois, *Fidel Castro*. New York: Bobbs-Merrill Company, Inc., 1959. As a correspondent for the *Chicago Tribune*, Dubois covered the *Bogotazo* in Bogotá in 1948. His early biography of Fidel helps to round out Fidel's image when considered with more recent works.

Carlos Franqui, *Family Portrait with Fidel: A Memoir*. New York: Random House, 1984. Franqui, the diarist of the Cuban Revolution, writes of Fidel from the viewpoint of one of the original *Fidelistas*. An intimate remembrance of Fidel and his followers.

Robert F. Kennedy, *Thirteen Days: A Memoir of the Cuban Missile Crisis*. New York: W.W. Norton & Company, 1969. This book reads like a suspense thriller. Kennedy provides a firsthand account of the thirteen-day event that brought the world to the edge of nuclear disaster.

Lee Lockwood, *Castro's Cuba, Cuba's Fidel: An American Journalist's Inside Look at Today's Cuba—In Text and Picture*. New York: MacMillan Company, 1967. This book is dated but still affords the reader a fascinating glimpse of the extraordinary relationship shared by Castro and the Cuban people.

Frank Mankiewicz and Kirby Jones, *With Fidel: A Portrait of Castro and Cuba*. New York: Ballantine Books, 1975. This is the account of the authors' visit with Fidel in the mid-1970s. It helps to provide interested readers with a better picture of the evolving dictator.

José Luis Llovio-Menéndez, *Insider: My Life as a Revolutionary in Cuba*. Translated by Edith Grossman. New York: Bantam Books, 1988. This tale is the stuff espionage novels are spun from. It is the true story of the highest ranking civilian official in Castro's government to seek asylum in the United States.

Ruby Hart Phillips, *Cuba: Island of Paradox*. New York: McDowell, Obolensky, 1960. Phillips documents what it was like to be bureau chief of the *New York Times* in the early days of the Cuban Revolution. Well-written, informing, and exciting.

Haydée Santamaría, *Moncada*. Secaucus, NJ: Lyle Stuart, 1980. Written by one of only two women to take part in the Moncada attack, this book offers a rare, firsthand account of the event that gave a name to Castro's revolutionary movement.

Arthur M. Schlesinger Jr., *A Thousand Days: John F. Kennedy in the White House*. Boston: Houghton Mifflin Company, 1965. This is a chronicle of the Kennedy administration by Kennedy's former White House assistant, valuable for its insights into the Kennedy-Castro relationship.

Hugh S. Thomas et al., *The Cuban Revolution 25 Years Later*. Boulder: Westview Press, 1984. Three esteemed historians look at what the Cuban Revolution has accomplished over the course of a quarter-century.

Works Consulted

Robert B. Asprey, *War in the Shadows: The Guerrilla in History*, Vol. II. Garden City, NY: Doubleday & Company, Inc., 1975. A brief but interesting overview of Cuban guerrillas, from Moncada through the Sierra Maestra, to the death of Che Guevara.

Dino A. Brugioni, in Robert F. McCort, ed., *Eyeball to Eyeball: The Inside Story of the Cuban Missile Crisis.* New York: Random House, 1991. The definitive account of the Cuban Missile Crisis by an eyewitness member of the intelligence community.

Theodore Draper, *Castro's Revolution: Myths and Realities.* New York: Frederick A. Praeger, Inc., 1962.

————, *Castroism: Theory and Practice.* New York: Frederick A. Praeger, Inc., 1965. Early, critical accounts of Fidel Castro and the Cuban Revolution.

R. Ernest Dupuy and Trevor N. Dupuy, *The Encyclopedia of Military History.* New York: Harper & Row, Publishers, 1977. Chronology and brief accounts of Cuba and the Cuban Revolution.

Carlos Franqui, *Diary of the Cuban Revolution.* New York: The Viking Press, 1980. The story of the Cuban Revolution as seen through the eyes of participants, written in a journal format.

Georgie Anne Geyer, *Guerrilla Prince: The Untold Story of Fidel Castro.* Kansas City, MO: Andrews and McMeel, 1993. A revealing portrait of the dynamics of a dictator by an experienced reporter.

K.S. Karol, *Guerrillas in Power.* New York: Hill & Wang, 1970. A well-documented analysis of the Cuban Revolution's first decade.

Victor Marchetti and John D. Marks, *The CIA and the Cult of Intelligence.* New York: Alfred A. Knopf, 1974. An inside look at the CIA's role in Cuban affairs and the search for Che Guevara.

Herbert L. Matthews, *Fidel Castro.* New York: Simon and Schuster, 1969. One of the kinder biographies of Fidel Castro, written by a veteran war correspondent for the *New York Times*.

Michael J. Mazarr, *Semper Fidel: America & Cuba 1776-1988.* Baltimore: The Nautical & Aviation Publishing Company of America, Inc., 1988. An in-depth study of the long, stormy, love-hate relationship between the United States and Cuba.

Louis A. Pérez Jr., *Cuba Between Reform and Revolution.* New York: Oxford University Press, Inc., 1988. A scholarly study of Cuba from pre-Columbian times to the present.

Robert E. Quirk, *Fidel Castro.* New York: W.W. Norton & Company, Inc., 1993. A recent biography written in exciting prose. In great detail, it tells the story of the man, the country, and the revolution.

Tad Szulc, *Fidel: A Critical Portrait.* New York: William Morrow and Company, Inc., 1986. A critical but fair portrayal of a man of many contradictions, and of the revolution he forged.

Robert Taber, *M-26: Biography of a Revolution.* New York: Lyle Stuart, 1961. One of the first books to be written about the Cuban Revolution. Informative. Reads like a novel.

Hugh Thomas, *The Cuban Revolution.* New York: Harper & Row, Publishers, 1977. The definitive work on the Cuban Revolution, through the middle of its second decade.

Robert Smith Thompson, *The Missiles of October: The Declassified Story of John F. Kennedy and the Cuban Missile Crisis.* New York: Simon and Schuster, 1992. A riveting recounting, day by day, hour by hour, of how President Kennedy faced his greatest crisis.

Fred Ward, *Inside Cuba Today.* New York: Crown Publishers, Inc., 1978. A comprehensive look at Cuba two decades after the revolution.

Peter Wyden, *Bay of Pigs: The Untold Story.* New York: Simon and Schuster, 1979. An exciting, well-written record of the Bay of Pigs fiasco, from concept to conclusion.

Index

Picture Credits

About the Author

Earle Rice Jr. learned about Cuba firsthand as a U.S. Marine stationed at Guantánamo Bay for twenty-seven months, just before the Batista coup. After his discharge, he attended San Jose City College and Foothill College on the San Francisco peninsula. He has authored eight previous books for young adults, including adaptations of *Dracula* and *All Quiet on the Western Front*. He has also written articles and short stories, and has previously worked for several years as a technical writer. Mr. Rice recently retired from the aerospace industry, where he worked as a senior design engineer. He lives in Julian, California, with his wife, daughter, granddaughter, two cats, and a dog.